Cryp

The Essential Guide to the Loch Ness Monster

(Compendium of North American Cryptids & Magical Creatures)

Danny Avalos

Published By **John Kembrey**

Danny Avalos

All Rights Reserved

Cryptids: The Essential Guide to the Loch Ness Monster (Compendium of North American Cryptids & Magical Creatures)

ISBN   978-1-77485-714-4

No part of this guidebook shall be reproduced in any form without permission in writing from the publisher except in the case of brief quotations embodied in critical articles or reviews.

Legal & Disclaimer

The information contained in this ebook is not designed to replace or take the place of any form of medicine or professional medical advice. The information in this ebook has been provided for educational & entertainment purposes only.

The information contained in this book has been compiled from sources deemed reliable, and it is accurate to the best of the Author's knowledge; however, the Author cannot guarantee its accuracy and validity and cannot be held liable for any errors or omissions. Changes are periodically made to this book. You must consult your doctor or get professional medical advice before using any of the suggested remedies, techniques, or information in this book.

Upon using the information contained in this book, you agree to hold harmless the Author from and against any damages, costs, and expenses, including any legal fees potentially resulting from the application of any of the information provided by this guide. This disclaimer applies to any damages or injury caused by the use and application, whether directly or indirectly, of any advice or information presented, whether for breach of contract, tort, negligence, personal injury, criminal intent, or under any other cause of action.

You agree to accept all risks of using the information presented inside this book. You need to consult a professional medical practitioner in order to ensure you are both able and healthy enough to participate in this program.

Table Of Contents

Introduction

Zoology is among the most fascinating and challenging fields of science. Even with all the technological advances and surveillance tools 2/3 of the planet is still a mystery. Every year in the jungles and ocean's depths, but they are it is also closer to home. Every expedition can uncover something previously unknown or newly developed There's a particular species of mosquito that is only found within underground tunnels like the London Underground.

However, more intriguingly there are a lot of species that are only known by the stories of legends or eyewitness reports. Without evidence that is concrete, scientists cannot declare them to be genuine animals, even though our history suggests that many of them are definitely. In the meantime, until evidence can be found However, they're classified as cryptids, and the hunt for them is called cryptozoology. Certain of them are examples of misidentification or a species may appear completely different under the right circumstances. Some are definitely fakes. However, the excitement of discovering the discovery of a new species and perhaps

1

being a part of the historical record as the one who proved the existence of it, has many individuals searching for the cryptids. Many of them invest massive sums of money and commit many years to this quest, while others diligently seek out data from books and on the internet, and then put it together with the intention of uncovering an answer in the puzzle.

Certain cryptids are famous; Bigfoot and the Loch Ness Monster are among the most well-known, as are the many other apemen as well as lake monsters found in folklore all over the globe. Other cryptids are less well-known and, in many cases, more bizarre. This book will examine ten cryptids which are, for the most part an actual possibility as well as explore the history and the science behind these mysterious creatures. In the pages to follow, you'll find frightening predators, potential survivors of dinosaurs, as well as beings which science cannot even begin to comprehend. Certain of them are located in a tiny, area; while others may appear everywhere in the world. What they share is the fact that lots of people believe in the existence of these animals and want to locate the single piece of evidence to show zoologists they're on the right track.

A lot of skeptical people are awestruck by their work by cryptozoologists and often they're right to do it. Sky squids, as an instance, is hard to accept as a fact. Horses aren't carnivores, don't exist in water and aren't able to transform into human forms and so the kelpie from Scottish legends is probably not worthy of being taken seriously. Sometimes, the stories of mysterious creatures can't be dismissed so easily . In some cases even today it's the cryptozoologists that are confirmed right and mainstream scientists that need to alter their theories and, in most cases they're happy to do. The purpose for this guide is to examine the cryptids that might be in the wild and discover the nature of what they could be. It's sure to be an exciting trip.

Chapter 1: Akkorukamai

The roots of the Japanese Ainu people are somewhat elusive. Many anthropologists believe that they're descendants of an ancient civilization who inhabited the islands for hundreds of years before their ancestors, the Yamato tribe, the people who rule Japan in the present, arrived. Nowadays, they reside mostly on the northern islands, Hokkaido as well as some scattered Russian islands located in the Sea of Okhotsk. Over the years, their relationships with the mainstream Japan were not always easy. In isolation, they needed to be self-sufficient with food and became skilled hunters and farmers. Their true talent was fishing, however. Inland villages were usually located near rivers, in which the sought-after Pacific salmon would be caught. In addition, coastal Ainu harvested a hefty harvest from the ocean. Utilizing flimsy boats that were about ten or fifteen feet in length, they hunted the biggest marine mammals and fish.

One of the largest Ainu fishing areas were Funka Bay. Its size is around twenty miles and surrounded by towering volcanoes, the body of water is alive with. Tuna and swordfish swim into the open ocean to feed. The fur seals as well as pilot whales also are attracted to the area. For the Ainu the Bay was appealing because it was a place to hunt the biggest quarry without having to face the dangers from the sea's open waters. However, perhaps the gray-colored surfaces of Funka Bay hid dangers of its own.

Why Funka Bay was so full of seals, fish, and whales was because it was filled with food. It's now heavily polluted, and in the summer months, level of oxygen within the waters can decrease dramatically, transforming the water into a dead pit however, prior to the 1990s there were huge groups of squid. They're an easy prey for seal or swordfish, and which is why predators would gather to feast on them. The Ainu devoured the predators. They soon discovered they were not the only ones hunting.

Funka Bay itself is shallow warm, clear water, the majority of it being under 200 feet of depth. Outside of its mouth however, the ocean floor gradually slopes down the continental shelf and into the cold, dark depths that lie in the North Pacific. Anything can rise from those depths and then move to the bay, and there are plenty of intriguing things that can be found in the depths of the ocean.

Sometime in the past - it's difficult to pinpoint precisely when however it was probably centuries back it was centuries ago that Ainu fishermen started returning to the bay telling tales of a frightful, nebulous creature. It was massive as they claimed and some accounts put it at as much as 400 feet in size. It had massive eyes and a glowing red body with long legs. Sometimes , it would attack fishing vessels. If fishermen cut the limb by using spears and knives, the monster could break it but it will always regenerate. Some fishermen started carrying large sickles in order to protect themselves from the beast, but the main danger was that the water that was displaced by the monster's massive weight would swamp their small boats. Whatever the reason the result was terrifying.

"And I saw in front of me an enormous and red swell beneath the waves. I initially thought my eyes were deceiving me and that I was simply seeing the reflection of the sun on the water, however as I walked closer I saw that it was a massive beast that was at least

80 metres (262 feet) in length at the very least as well as massive tentacles that were as large around as the torso of a man. The creature sat me down with its huge looking eye, before sinking into the depths and was sucked out of view."

The Ainu called the monster Akkorukamai and it was an integral part of their folklore about the sea. The tales eventually were incorporated onto Japanese culture and were incorporated into the Shinto religion. Akkorukamai was transformed into an Kami or spirit. Akkorukamai is believed to possess healing powers due to its ability to regenerate lost arms, however it's also a risk.

A traditional Ainu representation of Akkorukamai.

The legend of Akkorukamai is supported with more Ainu myths. In 1877, an English Missionary named John Batchelor, went to live with Ainu. Ainu and stayed for the following 64 years. The traditional Ainu language and culture are in decline, being to be replaced by modern Japanese ones. Batchelor's diaries and essays are among the top sources of information about the way they lived. In his book of 1901 The Ainu and their Folk-Lore he described the appearance and appearance of Akkorukamai:

"In the early morning we discovered the entire village in clouds. Three men, according to the story were on their way to catch swordfish. However, suddenly a huge sea monster with huge looking eyes, appeared right before them and then attacked the boat. A desperate fight ensued. The beast was round and released the dark, noxious scent. Three men fled in awe and astonishment, but not because of fear, as they claim however, due to the horrible smell. Whatever the reason it, they were terrified that the next day they were unable to get up and take a meal; they lay on their beds, pale and shaking."

There are sufficient indications within the descriptions for Akkorukamai to make a pretty good guess that it's a cephalopod. The mollusc family includes octopi, cuttlefish and squid. All of them possess characteristics which are consistent with Ainu legends. Cephalopods are characterized by tentacles (and are often able to regrow them) They can also spray dark ink, and a lot of them have huge eyes. Cuttlefish aren't ruled out however, as they're tiny with the biggest species growing less than 2 feet in length. This implies that Akkorukamai is either a squid , or an Octopus. The majority of them are small however, there are exceptions. Certain of them are extremely large, and they've also been the basis of numerous myths regarding sea monsters. The legendary Kraken for instance, could be only a giant Octopus.

The most famous cephalopods known are squid. The giant squid has been featured many times in the world of fiction including J.R.R. Tolkien's 20,000 Leagues under the Sea to Jaws author Peter Benchley's Beast. It's depicted as a massive and terrifying creature, with the body measuring thirty feet or more and a total length of between sixty and eighty feet. This isn't as huge as the famous Akkorukamai however, it's still an enormous animal. However, the reality isn't exactly matching to the myth, however. The squid's massive size can be more than 40 feet but nearly two-thirds is tentacles. The body itself is generally between six and 15 feet in length and can weigh around 600 ponds. It's massive, but when in comparison to other creatures that we've seen living in the ocean, it's not as big. It doesn't quite match the descriptions of what could be lurking at the bottom of Funka Bay.

The fact is that giant squids aren't understood as well since very few have been studiedand up until recently our ignorance was never complete. Scientists debated over the size they got as well as the length of their tentacles and arms were and what the tentacles were equipped with. All agreed they had been covered by strong suckers that were used to grasp prey, however some claimed the suckers were ringed by teeth. Others claimed that they had hook claws at the center. Some even claimed they had both. Each group had evidence to prove this, but none was conclusive. In 1981, an Russian trawler in Antarctica discovered a huge squid that measured 13 feet in length. The tentacles it had were identical to two of them discovered inside the stomach of a whale sperm in 1925, however they were not as large as the squid's tentacles of a huge one. This was when scientists realized there was a different, larger, species that they had only thought of prior to.

What they discovered was a brand new animal much larger than the giant squid. In a rare display of scientific humor, it was swiftly identified as the colossal Squid and it's a good description. In terms of overall length, it's not as large as a gigantic squid. The squid is believed to measure 46 feet as opposed to 43 feet for its squid cousin - however, it's got a larger body. The mantle (the bullet-shaped piece which heads are connected to) can be up to 14 feet, compared to around nine feet for the giant. Furthermore, it's also a lot heavier. The largest squid ever caught is 33 feet and weighed more than half a tonne, but in light of the dimensions of the beaks inside whale stomachs, a huge one could have twice the weight. The body of the colossal squid is more like an acorn rather than a bullet. This corresponds to its description as Akkorukamai with a body that is round, and there are additional similarities. The skin of the squid is a dark red hue and it also has the biggest eyes of any animal that can reach 16 inches in size. It's also a far more deadly animal as it turned out that scientists who claimed that giant squid had claws were correct - however, it was the massive Squid that had claws. Each sucker features a terrifying spike at the center, similar to a gigantic cat's claw, which can reach two inches in length, which allow it to grasp prey and cause painsome wounds.

The massive squid may be huge and strong, but it's not exactly a fierce predator. It has a low metabolic rate, and despite its massive size, only requires 1 ounce of food per day. Scientists believe they're an ambush predator that lurks in the depths, using its large eyes to detect any activity, before launching some of the tentacles on its lengthy whip in order to take it away. It feeds on fish, smaller squids and other invertebrates. It does not feed daily. In turn , it's eaten by Sperm whales. It isn't known how widespread the colossal sea squid is, but it's not uncommon as a result of examinations of the stomachs of sperm whales,, colossal squid comprise three-quarters their intake of food. There are hundreds of thousands of Sperm whales in the world and each consumes over an ounce of food every day, meaning there must be millions of the colossal Squid.

That's certainly the reason the fishermen from Funka Bay thought Akkorukamai could regenerate its arms. They might have seen the same squid on a regular basis. It's possible that the Funka Bay monster's aggressive behavior isn't exactly in line with our knowledge of massive squid however. It's not what ambush predators are doing, and the colossal fish lives below the surface in cold waters and doesn't appear to be a fan of warmer water on the surface and every specimen taken has been brought up from a distance of thousands of feet under the sea surface. It's not likely that they'd frequent Funka Bay.

Some have speculated that Akkorukamai might be an octopus, and not an squid, however that isn't likely. The most well-known member of the family is the massive Pacific octopus. But that's not nearly as big as the squid that is massive. The largest specimen that has ever been seen was only 300 pounds, and had arms that, spread and extending 32 feet from end to end. It's an enormous octopus that could prove to be a terrifying foe for a diver , but it's not like the one that Ainu are familiar with. There is always the possibility that larger oceanic octopi are present, of course. The majority of them are marine creatures, but the huge Pacific octopus is found in the ocean floor down to 6,600 feet deep. There are larger ones that could be hiding into the depths. It's not likely, however since even though fragments of the large squid were found prior to the species being identified, the last Octopus bigger than the GPO was ever discovered.

Akkorukamai could not be a gigantic sea squid or huge Pacific Octopus however, it's definitely something. There are too many reports of it over a lengthy period to believe it's an elaborate hoax or the product of one's imagination. Additionally, unlike many cryptids, such as that of the Loch Ness Monster and Loch Ness Monster, the encounters aren't just glimpses of something that seems to be from a distance. The creature has fought boatsand has been wounded by the weapons of fishermen. It's definitely a cethalopod of some sort, however the question is what. Perhaps it's a massive version of the aggressive Humboldt squid, or perhaps an other species that hasn't been discovered in the past? This is the most likely scenario.

Chapter 2: Terrors Of The Deep Lazarus Sharks

The giant cephalopods aren't all the problems lurking in the deep ocean. In 1898, a grotesque shark was captured close to Yokohama, Japan. It was not huge at 42 inches however it was later discovered to be an unadulterated goblin shark. A little research revealed that the goblin shark was recognized in Japan for several years due to occasional captures by startled fishermen. However, for the first time, western scientists started to study the shark.

It was an unusual creature. A mature goblin is huge typically around 12 feet in length, but can reach up to twenty feet. It is characterized by an snout that is sword-like, flat and jaws that can extend, conjuring an image of the hungry monster from Alien. It's also pretty harmless. small and weak in comparison to the size of it, but swam slowly and hunts smaller fish as well as Squid. The skin of the fish is dark gray-pink hue, as it doesn't require camouflage as it is deep, typically between the 900-3,000 feet mark beneath the surface, and in waters with pressures that exceed 1.300 pounds/square inch. Its surroundings are completely dark , aside from the tiny, glowing spots of bioluminescent creatures. Goblin sharks aren't blind, but its eyes aren't big and hunts by smell as well as the electronic sensors that line its long nose.

Goblin shark. Image created by Hungarian Snow. Image used under the Creative Commons 2.0 License

The most interesting thing regarding the goblin shark the fact that it's also the last shark to survive from a family that existed in the Cretaceous period, which was 120 millennia ago. Fossils have revealed a variety of goblin species, but only one species, Mitsukurina Owstoni, appears to be a relic. The living fossil, one of the last survivors from the ancient times.

Of course , in a sense sharks of all kinds are old. Sharks, as well as skates and rays, don't look unlike other fish. The first fish was seen around 5 million years ago, and they had boney skeletons similar to vertebrates nowadays. However, during the Devonian period, about the time of 420 million something odd took place. Certain types of fish slowly lost their bones, and replaced them with strong, elastic cartilage. As an evolutionary test, it wasn't an extremely effective one, as bony fishes are now dominant in both fresh and marine waters however some cartilaginous species have survived and continue to grow. Most impressive are pelagic sharks which are the most powerful predators that inhabit the ocean. Mako or Tiger shark is an evolved creature that has been completely adapted to its surroundings It's clear that it's distinct from the typical fish. When bony and cartilaginous fish divergedaround 200 million years prior to the emergence of dinosaurs, the sole distinction between them was their skull. Since then, bony fish have evolved as rapidly like land mammals. They've gotten features such as the ability to swim bladder that will maintain them at a constant depth without burning calories as well as movable gill flaps that allow an unstoppable circulation of oxygen-rich water. Sharks, despite their long-standing roots aren't equipped with these capabilities. They need to swim for a long time otherwise they'll sink to bottom and, without flow of water over their gills and die. While they've changed over the years passed by, with old species changing into new species as well as dying away, the fundamental structure of sharks hasn't changed much since their long-lost predecessors.

The goblin shark's experience is that it's not only the fundamental attributes that have survived the test of time; there are some ancient species that are found in the oceans. The goblin of today isn't identical to one that existed one hundred million years ago, of course and its immune system is now able to handle modern parasites and diseases, and its teeth as well as the digestive tract has been adjusted to the types of prey they encounter in our oceans. However, despite these minor modifications, it's identified as the same animal. It raises the question: what else could have been able to survive?

The shark with the highest apprehension and the most frightening creature, perhaps - that has ever existed roamed oceans in the Cenozoic period. Fossils have been discovered that date between 15.9 and 2.6 millennia ago. which means it was an extremely recent species than the goblin shark. The megalodon was the fish that was found.

Carcharadon megalodon first came to light by fossilized teeth around 1835. The most intriguing aspect for researchers was the fact that the teeth they examined were very similar to those of living animals however, they were much bigger. The living species was known as the Great White shark, Carcharadon carcharias. The great white can grow to more than 20 feet long and is capable of swimming at speeds up to 35 mph. It only has one predator in the natural world which is the killer whale and is known as a man-eater. It is the biggest of sharks that devour almost anything that is in the ocean, cutting its prey into chunks using an array of over 200 sharp, serrated teeth. These teeth measure around two inches in length when you're the adult stage and each is a powerful triangular blade that is capable of cutting through flesh and breaking bones. The researchers discovered that the fossils had similar in shape and also had serrated edges similar to those however, they were significantly larger with about seven inches in length. In the event that similar teeth originated from the same animal, it could indicate that the shark was eighty feet long.

Since then, many more megalodon teeth have been discovered. Teeth are generally the only fossils left from sharks due to the fact that unlike bone, cartilaginous skeleton can be consumed by bacteria once an animal is killed. Sometimes, scientists have been lucky, however. Vertebral centrum - a part that comprise the spine column are the most long-lasting remnants of a dead shark , and sometimes , they're hidden before microbes take them away. Then , they transform into fossils. In 1926, about 150 centra were discovered close to Antwerp in Belgium Twenty more were discovered within Denmark at the time of 1983. It's evident by these fossils that although megalodon wasn't quite identical to the great white, it was closely similar. The two species were sea-bound and the oldest fossils of the great white are believed to be 16 million years old.

Based on fossils and more recently, using computer models scientists have recreated what the megalodon might have looked like. It's a terrifying image. While it's possible that it wasn't so big as some estimates claimed, it was nevertheless massive, with a spindle-like, streamlined body that was between fifty and sixty feet and a mass of over 50 tons. It was

21

much more built as compared to the white, particularly its huge head, which contained jaws that were up to the width of eight feet. These jaws would have been covered with more than 200 massive teeth, and the force of the teeth indicates an enormous bite force. It's logical, since fossil whale bones show gouge marks that match the megalodon's teeth, and it would have required a strong bite to kill the massive creatures. Remains of a 30 foot whale reveal that megalodon fought by grabbing its victim in the chest, then crushing its internal organs as well as its ribs. Certain small whales may be rammed from below at high speeds and this would have stunned them , making them easily killed - Great whites hunt seals precisely this manner. Similar to adult great whites, the megalodon appears to have mainly eaten mammals, however anything that was within its range of detection was acceptable game. Even whales that were larger than it were targets. The megalodon would cut off their flippers and tails or just wait for them to be drowned or killed by chewing off huge pieces of flesh. There's evidence to suggest that the raptorial sperm whale the biggest predatory mammal found in the ocean of the past was part of the megalodon's diet.

Megalodon jaw. Image created by James St. John and licensed by permission under CC 2.0 License. 2.0 License

Researchers believe that approximately 2.6 million years earlier,, megalodon became extinct. There aren't any fossils that are older than this one have been discovered and there's never been any reliable evidence of a living specimen. The most likely explanation could be that when the seas cool down, plankton was less prevalent and whales, megalodon's preferred food source - decreased along with the temperature. In the absence of food sources, the great sharks went extinct.

Did they? A biologist has never seen megalodons, but there are some evidence that suggests they might be able to survive. HMS Challenger was an Royal Navy corvette, converted into a survey vessel and embarked on a mission for exploration, in 1872. The goal was to discover the depths of the ocean. She carried a total of 181 miles of rope dragging the sea bed. The deepest trench ever discovered, Challenger Deep, off the Mariana

Islands, is named for her. In the month of March 1875, she dug the weight of a lead more than five miles beneath the ocean, which was the deepest ocean ever discovered in that time. In actual fact, the weight fell in the middle of the trench. The most bottom part, which is only about a hundred yards further and seven miles below.

Moving on through the Pacific Challenger was able to discover a deeper trench close to Tahiti. One of the goals of the mission was to discover what's living on the ocean floor, and so the ship frequently dragged in a net made of steel along the sea's bottom. In her 70,000-mile voyage, she collected thousands of species which included more than 4000 species that had never ever been seen before. Today on Tahiti the net brought two megalodon teeth.

In the meantime, a number of teeth were found, and the megalodon was not unknown, therefore the teeth weren't causing any excitement. The situation changed in 1959 when professor W. Tschernezky tested the layer of chemical that had formed over them and found that it could take as short 10000 years old. It's an eternity to us, but in the realm of geological time it's just the blink of an eye. If megalodon could have been able to survive the Plesitocene cooling, they might still be around. Since then, more studies have been conducted but the results aren't conclusive. There's not enough carbon in the teeth to be able to offer a definitive answer , and the majority of scientists believe that the teeth are much longer old than Tschernezky believed, but they may not be.

In 1918, David Stead, an Australian naturalist who wrote about an event which had terrified fishermen at Port Stephens on the coast of New South Wales. There was a bustling local lobster trade that revolved on Broughton Islands. Broughton Islands, a tiny piece of land located only two miles off shore Local boats set off each day for the waters deep around Broughtons to set traps. Broughtons to set traps. In the summer of 1918, while raising their traps the shark swam before three men. It was a ghostly white shark as the men claimed that it was massive; estimates were ranging from 115-300 feet! It's evident that there's a significant exaggeration here, but it's normal when people are scared by a shark, and the fishermen were. In fact, for three days, they refused to go out to sea even though it meant they were unable to earn a living. The shark did not attack their vessels, but instead swam towards the traps, instead taking them off the sea bed and then swallowing the traps. Each trap was three and five feet wide and was constructed from the frame of a wooden weighted frame, which was then with nets. Sharks devour indigestible objects often and the tiger shark is often referred to as "the garbage bin of the ocean" because of the rubbish that is located in its stomachs - and a megalodon is able to swallow a trap, eat its contents and then digest the rest.

Fishermen are fond of telling stories about their fish, but the fact those from Port Stephens ones wouldn't go back out to sea suggests that something was really happening out on the Broughton Islands. Stead talked to the fisheries inspector in the area who said that only a large and frightening creature could have scared off fishermen to such an extent. It's interesting to note that this story did not originate from a single individual It was the result of a team of skilled mariners.

Western Author Zane Grey and his son both claimed that they saw megalodons in the

1920s and the early 1930s, but the 40-foot creature they mentioned was evidently the whale shark. It's not the same about a common sighting just a few decades afterward. It has the odor of a urban legend since it's difficult to locate any specific details about it about what happened "in the early 1960s" in the 1960s and "on the edge of the Great Barrier Reef". When an 85-foot fishing vessel was anchored in order to solve an engine problem , an enormous white shark spotted itself and swam slowly close to the boat, when the crew noticed the shark was larger that the vessel. It was clearly not a whale shark in the event that the story is real.

Both of these stories originate from Australia and there are constant reports of vessels around the Great Barrier Reef finding minor damaged hulls, often with tooth fragments wedged into their plating. This occurs when they collide with a massive underwater object. It is true that the Great Barrier Reef is in fairly shallow waters and coral requires sunlight to grow , but just a few miles into the ocean, the bed of the sea recedes quickly into the depths of the depths of the abyss.

Also, there are accounts from Americas. In 1930, fishermen of Grand Manan in the Gulf of Maine reported on catching and killing a great white of 37 feet that had attacked a boat owned by the locals. In the following years, fishermen who were fishing on the Gulf of Mexico sometimes wrote about a 30-foot shark who was seen circling their vessels. Sometimes, it would eat their entire nets when they hauled them into the water. Other times, it preyed upon dolphins and other sharks that accompanied fishing vessels. There are, however, newer sightings as well.

In the past couple of years, fishermen within the Sea of Cortez have begun discussing what they call"the Black Demon, an enormous shark that is ravaging the waters. It's three times the size as the largest great white, a species that you've heard of and is prey on marine mammals such as sea lions and small whales. There are some experts who believe that it's a whale shark they can grow to 40 feet in length. This is more than the great white however, it's not a harmful plankton eater. If the fish that is causing all the trouble is actually eating sea lions, it isn't the whale shark. However, the fishermen say it is.

Carcasses have been found to have massive pieces of flesh that have been ripped out.

In contrast to Australian sightings, the Sea of Cortez shark is said to be dark in the color. Of course , we don't know what color megalodon actually was, but the great white could be an accurate indication. Despite its name , most part of it is dark gray shaded by white in the lower belly and flanks. One possibility is that Australians observed the underside of the shark - sharks are known to are known to roll over their backs while feeding or when they display aggression.

The sightings of The Sea of Cortez continue. In 2008, Eric Mack's fishing boat was struck by something huge inside the Sea. The tail of the animal was five feet higher than the surface of the ocean This rule out the possibility of a whale as their Tail flukes have a horizontal shape. It is believed that the Sea of Cortez is a heavily fished area, but nets and lines generally remain in the upper hundred feet. In some areas, the seabed swells away to 9,800 feet or higher nearly two miles deep.

It is possible that a remnant population of megalodon might be able to survive? The majority of scientists think that the great predator is gone however the answer seems to be yes, it's possible. Similar to the great white megalodon, the great white preferred cooler waters of the coastal plains However, the great whites are showing to be much more adaptable than biologists believed. It's now understood that they can dive up to 2000 feet to search for prey. They are able to survive and stay active even in freezing depths, due to the fact that unlike sharks they are able to keep their bodies at temperatures higher than that of the water they swim in. Mako sharks, which are close to both the megalodon and great white have the same capability, and it's probable that megalodon also did also. This means that it might remain alive if it shifted away from the shore and into the deep ocean deep.

The night that never ends under the ocean, extending beyond the continental shelf, where the bottom falls rapidly to a depth of two and quarter miles is a jarring and unexplored area. Only a tiny fraction of the depth has been explored. It seems crazy, but we have more knowledge on the planet's surface Mars than the surface of our planet. There are many species there that we've observed but we know very little about. The most well-known is the Megamouth Shark. an eerie 18-foot plankton eater that was largely undiscovered until the time a US Navy ship hauled up an unidentified dead shark entangled in its anchor at sea in the year 1976.

Do megalodons go without being noticed in the darkness? It's a clear yes. It may have had excellent eyesight, but it wouldn't require to be hunting by. sharks have organs - called the Ampullae of Lorenzini which detect electromagnetic disturbances. In the great white, they're able enough to detect the electrical pulses that accompany the heart beating. There's plenty of food for such huge predators. The predators down there tend to grow to an enormous size and be a deep-diving whale's food source. Megalodons can live their entire life in the abyss and never meet the human race.

But there's something to take into consideration. If the shark that is the greatest is in the depths, it's because the shark was driven to the area to hunt for food some time ago, due to the cooling oceans. Sea temperatures are increasing steadily, at 1.5deg F over the last century. What happens if megalodon appears once more?

Chapter 3: Black Dog

It's one of our primal fears, a nightmare that can trace our roots to our ancestors from the African plains. At night, alone, suddenly, there's a loud sharp snarl, a throaty snarl, and huge black silhouette emerges out of the darkness. For the majority of people, who fear darkness, it's the fear of what could be lurking in the darkness... looking for us... making preparations to start the spring. Over the years, the ancestral stories of predators real and imaginary have been weaved into the folklore of our time, and nowhere are these myths more pervasive that in Britain.

There aren't any large predators that are left in Britain in the present. The lynx was extinct by the 6th century. The last English predators were killed in the 16th century, but they survived in Scotland for about 200 years more or less. The largest carnivore native to the United States is the badger. Although the area may be free of wild beasts, but the mythology isn't, and the most well-known as well as striking among these mythological animal species is the black dog.

Black dogs are featured in the folklore of every region in the United Kingdom. There is no way to determine if the stories originated in the UK or were brought to it from Germanic or Norse invaders. However, giant supernatural animals certainly were present in Celtic mythology. The Cwn Annwn, or Hounds of the Otherworld they guarded the entry point to the afterlife in the ancient pagan religion. This is very similar to the myth of Cerberus the three-headed dog that prevented dead people from going to their ancient Greek underworld. Norse mythology has the same creature in Garmr, the guard dog of Hel (the Norse Hel was not the same as the Christian Hell It appears to be a place that people would have wanted to visit after death, and it could have had a similarity in some ways to Valhalla).

Wherever the legend originated, it's deeply rooted in the history of. From the tchen Bodu as well as the headless Tchico located in the Channel Islands, to the cow-sized Cu Sith of the Scottish Highlands, the stories are all over the place. Scandinavian examples are most likely an ancient remnant of Norse mythology. They've been transported to USA, Canada and Argentina by British migrants , and have popped up all over all across the North Sea in Flanders and northern Germany. They can be seen in Croatia as well as Italy. Most spectral dogs are large and bright eyes (apart from the ones that are headless). They're typically associated with death , and often it's the demise of the one that sees them.

Black dog stories have found their way to popular culture. For instance, the Sherlock Holmes tale The Hound of the Baskervilles is perhaps the most well-known instance. It is based on a Dartmoor legend of an huntsman who struck an arrangement to the Devil. Then, after his death, the there were black dogs roaming in the vicinity of his tomb. In the last few years, The Harry Potter books picked up on two other unknown creatures. in The Prisoner of Azkaban Harry is worried that he's being followed by Grim. Grim Later, it turns out his father Sirius Black, who can transform into a massive dog, is known as Padfoot. Grim or Padfoot can be both Lancashire nicknames for the ghostly dogs. There are many more names, with the majority of them referring to specific areas. Some aren't very imaginative like The Black Dog Of Bouley Bay and the Black Dog Of Newgate and Black Dogs Of many other locations. Other are more distinctive and one of the most well-known are Black Shuck.

The most famous black dogs are feared creatures due to their connection with death. Black Shuck, though, is believed to be dangerous. According to the legends of Suffolk the flat mist-haunted region along the England's North Sea coast, are stories of Shuck taking his victims with his throats, causing deadly consequences.

Black Shuck's legend Black Shuck goes back at minimum to the 13th century. However, the most frightening tale happened more than a decade later. It's reported in a report written by one Anglican clergyman who claimed that on the 4th of August 1577, during a service of worship in the Holy Trinity Church in Blythburgh the dog of a massive black abruptly swarmed through the church and swam into the congregation. The dog killed a man and one boy before running out and returning to the church, where a raging storm was in full force. Then, hours later, it appeared on St Mary's Church in Bungay just 12 miles away. It again attacked two people who were there, and "wrung the necks of both".

Many black dogs are believed with supernatural abilities, however Shuck was a rare instance. Shuck's appearance in Blythburgh in addition to Bungay was closely connected to the day's thunderstorm and many were of the opinion the belief that Shuck might be Devil himself. The Reverend Fleming's story claims that the enormous dog was surrounded by flames when he began his attacks. The enigmatic doorways made of wood in Holy Trinity Church still bear scorch marks believed as having been left behind by the claws of the monster.

Evidently, fiery hellhounds reside within the realm of mythology, not science and scorch marks could have a myriad of explanations. Historical researchers have attempted to discover alternatives to the brutal deaths that took place in Suffolk. The 16th century ended in an era of religious war in England and being a time of conflict with the Protestant reformation pitting the newly formed Church of England against the older Catholic religion. Elizabeth I, Queen Elizabeth I was determined to unite the nation and sought to find a compromise between the extreme European Protestants and traditional English Catholic worship. As such, she helped steer the newly formed Anglican church towards a type which was suitable to both parties. This wasn't a good thing for all however. There were those who believed that the Puritans are extremists that believed that reforms hadn't progressed enough and that every trace from Roman Catholicism should be rooted out. There were the non-regenerate Catholic priests who refused to recognize an elected monarch to be the head of the Church, instead of the pope. Elizabeth was a wise and patient leader, but her patience was not endless. In 1575, the Archbishop of Canterbury published a lengthy anti-Puritan essay that was highly negative of Elizabeth and was promptly removed and sent to life imprisonment in a house. Then European priests began to appear and the idea of an "underground" Catholic church started to appear. Religion was a very political issue , and the question of who would have the ultimate authority over Britain - the crown or the pope is a contentious one. It was not long before the protests against the Anglican settlement was pushed to treason and demands for the overthrow of House of Tudor. Elizabeth was done with it and executions of priests who had rebelled began.

The English Reformation was nowhere near as brutal as the religious wars which destroyed Continental Europe, and the oppression by clergymen Catholic clergy was restricted to a handful of the most violent agitators, however it was still extremely painful for many who secretly backed the pope. It is significant to note that this was the year in which the first priest was executed - 1577. Suffolk is located at the heart of East Anglia, where the violence was at its most severe and could the story of the infamous, deadly black dog that attacked the churches be a reference to Elizabeth's reforms? This is what historians believed - but they're mistaken.

Leiston Abbey, eight miles south of Blythburgh it was founded in 1182. It became an influential Augustinian monastery. Henry VIII suppressed the monastic orders , however, and in the 1530s , it was confiscated and handed over to the Earl of Suffolk. The Earl of Suffolk constructed a farmhouse on the site , and the chapel that was deteriorating became an agricultural barn. The farmhouse today is meticulously maintained and remains the centre of a farm that is in operation, however it's an unfinished shell. In the past, the fact the farm was a farm didn't mean that anyone considered it to be an archeological site. However, in 2013, a group of researchers selected to use it as the venue for an experiment in public-funded archaeology. It's always been difficult to raise money to finance an excavation, but DigVentures decided to test crowdfunding. In exchange for donating , members of the public could be allowed to help excavat the site under the direction and guidance by experts. The project was a huge accomplishment and soon, artefacts started to appear and include evidence of a prehistoric settlement at the site, something that historians had never thought about.

Then, someone spotted the dog.

When the team was removing the dirt's first layer from a trench that was newly dug an axe smacked something solid. The dirt was then gently loosen and then brushed away, showing bones that were yellowed. They soon realized that it was the bone of a dog but not your typical dog. The beast was huge. The remains of the beast indicate that it was seven feet tall on its hind legs and may have weighed up to 200 pounds. It was buried in a grave that was less than two feet in depth, however pottery fragments found in the soil around it are believed to date from the late

16th century, which is approximately the timeframe of Black Shuck's brutal rampage.

The Leiston discovery suggests that the myth that surrounds Black Shuck could be based on actual events and not just a metaphor. It is possible that a massive dog actually exploded into two churches to attack the congregations. It's also possible the frightened crowds enhanced the tale to include an ethereal halo that resembled Satanic flames.

However, Black Shuck is just one of many massive black dogs that are believed to roam Britain and cannot all be tied neatly to an skull. There are so many similar stories dating back to time, and coming from a variety of locations across the country, it's like there's a lot of truth to the story. There's a possibility that the myth has its roots in the period where wolves were still roaming across the countryside, but it's not clear why the sightings continued to be reported long following the killing of the last wild wolf. Indeed, large animals , often black, continue to be reported across areas of the British countryside. These aren't dogs, however. They're cats.

A single of the more fascinating cryptids - one that most mainstream biologists believe do exist is the ABC or Alien Big Cat. Numerous eyewitnesses, including police officers or Royal Marines, have told of encounters with big cat-like creatures as well as a number of sightings are difficult to disprove. There's no doubt that large cats are free in Britain as they've been taken captive. In the year 1980, a mountain lion that could be a pet that was released that was caught in a cage trap close to Inverness, Scotland. Anther was killed and shot by an officer from Greenwich, London, in 1987. In 1991, the police of Norfolk which is located just north of Suffolk and which is where Black Shuck roamed - shot the body of an Eurasian lynx which was killing sheep. In 1994 William Rooker of Cambridgeshire - close to Suffolk recorded the video of two minutes of a black cat the size of a cougar wandering around the fields. The years 2003 and 2004, there over 2,000 sightings reported of large cats, with 17 in which the cat was with cubs. If any of the above are true, it means that there's more than the occasional pet that has escaped or zoo animals They're breeding.

Eurasian Lynx shot in Northern Ireland in the year 1996. Image taken by Royal Ulster Constabulary

The experts who believe that big cats live and breed on the British countryside usually believe that they are the descendants of animals released from their homes. In the years prior to 1976, it was legal to keep almost any animal that was an animal in the UK However, after the law changed, many pet owners weren't interested in dealing with the expense of papers and enclosure requirements. So instead as unbelievable as it sounds they let them roam free. At at least 23 large cats, including lynxes and cougars, and a leopard were released into the wild in the latter part of the 1970s, and the true amount is likely to be much greater.

There are those who doubt that big cats could wander around Britain and not be spotted However, that's not the case - they are being spotted with a frequency of around three or four sightings per day. The sheep have also been shot as well as horses, and even some people have been are being beaten. In 2005, a skull was discovered in Devon which experts determined to be belonging to an elusive coyote. It was interesting to note that this discovery was in the vicinity from one of Britain's most well known big cats Bodmin's Beast. Additionally, the Bodmin region has been known for centuries as the home of the black dog.

It is possible that some of these mysterious black dogs actually are big cats? At first , it appears unlikely, but it's really not too far-fetched in reality. The majority of people look at what they are expecting to see, and since the black dog is so firmly rooted in mythology, any large animal that is seen in the night when cats hunt however dogs don't hunt are likely to be seen as one. There are some intriguing clues. The traditional English pub signs haven't seen much change over the years and the design just being repainted as it fades. black dogs appear on many of them. Some of the dogs feature distinct feline characteristics, such as the eyes of a famous instance in Jersey.

Evidently, if even a few of these legends could be traced to large cats, then the cats that were released in 1976 aren't the cause, however there has been no big cats native to in Britain from before the end of the Ice Age.

What is their origin? This is a mystery that won't be solved. Perhaps they escaped of the Roman amphitheaters? What is the likelihood? The only thing that seems to be certain is that something's out there, running through the dark woods and lanes. And if you're located in Britain you could be the next one to experience it. What fun would that be?

Chapter 4: The Sleep Demons

Imagine the scenario. You awake suddenly in bed. It's late in the night, your space is nearly completely dark, and you're feeling a bit fuzzy and lost. You've awakened hundreds of occasions, however this time is something completely different. You try to wipe the sleep out of your eyes and get used to the idea of being awake but and then you realize that you're totally immobilized. However, it gets more severe. As your awareness begins to filter into your brain, you feel a threatening presence, possibly in the shadows of your eyes. You begin to feel a tension on your chest. It is slowly restricting your breathing. The mind is telling that it is in your chest. Something dangerous.

This terrifying story is the basis of numerous stories about alien encounters. People who have been victims believe that they've been viewed, questioned or even subjected to experiments by aliens. Many skeptical people accuse them of fabricating the story, but the evidence is uniform; it's difficult to believe that thousands of people could be able to come up with the exact identical story, unless there's a reason that is behind it.

46

The story isn't new, but. Take a look back and similar stories can be found, however, there were no references to aliens. Instead, a list of supernatural creatures were blamed with distinct regional differences in what was believed to be the source. Here are a few of the most commonly blamed suspects:

* Hag. "The word "hag" originates in"hag" which is the Old English word haegtasse, which means witch. In various myths, a "hag" may be a witch or a supernatural creature with the form of an elderly woman. In stories of attacks on sleepers, they're supernatural, they lie on the chest of the sleeping person and give them nightmares. If the person awakes, they're in a state of paralysis and cannot move, or even to call for assistance. Another term used to describe this kind of woman is a mare. That's where the term "nightmare" originates.

* Succubus. Succubus are female demons, or sexual vampire. They show up in the form of dreams, and entice their victims. The signs associated with an attack like those of a mare or the hag but with the exception that the victim is also reported as having a sexual encounter in the presence of the beast. It is

important to note that many reports of contemporary encounters with aliens in particular, where the person is sleeping when the encounter occurs, also contain sexual themes.

Traditionally, the succubus is depicted as a terrifying creature, however, there are some stories that depict the succubus as gorgeous women, but often with demonic traits like talons or tails. In modern fiction, they tend to be attractive, and this is some clues - vampires are also popularly romanticized in contemporary fiction which suggests that the traits of these night-time visitors are influenced by cultural.

The incubus is the male version of the succubus that selects female victims. In either case, frequent visits from the creature may cause illness , or even death.

* Vampire. In addition to the succubus or incubus, the more conventional vampire is often described as a nighttime visitor. It was during the Middle Ages most diagnoses of vampirism were reported following the death of the victim however some individuals have reported stories of attacks and paralysis was also the most frequent topic.

The succubus is an iconic image in the art of medieval times. Image created by anenomeproject, and licensed under the CC the 2.0 License

When you look at these myths What's striking is the degree to which they are linked with modern stories of alien encounters. It's easy to say that these stories all have the same origin and the various explanations coming from the changing influences of culture. It's also likely that the aliens had visited us for centuries. However, for a long period, people believed that the attacks were supernatural creatures rather than extraterrestrial ones. In other words, incubi and hags may still be causing trouble for people, but , now, having been conditioned by films and books about aliens, we are more likely to blame aliens from another world. The choice you choose is up to your own personal beliefs. If you're convinced that aliens are coming to us you'll likely prefer the first option, whereas fans of the dead are likely to choose the other. The thing that everyone agrees on is how the signs are similar to that no matter what the reason it's the same for both modern and traditional instances. Are we being afflicted by succubi or spacefarers?

Scientists think the solution could be "neither". Strange nocturnal creatures, not like many mythological animals, were documented across every culture and time period. It seems that the reason for this is due to something that we all do - sleeping.

Sleep is a complicated process. From the viewpoint of our conscious minds, things are just turned off and then come back on just a few hours later. Sometimes, we recall dreams that occur in the middle, however, they tend to disappear within a few minutes after waking. Up. We aren't aware of the world around us when we're asleep. We're not able to remember any details about it. It's just an interruption in consciousness. From the brain's perspective perception, there's more happening, however. There are several stages of sleep and we transition between them through the night.

When we are first settling down to sleep, the state is quite sluggish We still react to sounds and touch and some movement is perceived. Slowly, we begin to sink; brain activity alters and we lose our ability to respond. Within a half-hour, the previously erratic activity of the brain shifts to an array of slow, deep waves that appear clear on monitors. It's hard to wake someone in this state and, if you do, they'll feel groggy and confused. Sleeping in slow waves appears to be a time where the brain is recharged and is able to recover from the work that it has done during the day. It's a top priority and the brain is able to get rid of it within the first three hours after falling to sleep. Then you go back to a more restful but still refreshing state where you're not able to get up, but your the activity of your brain is greater than that of sleep at a slow rate. But about every 90 minutes through the entire cycle there's a change in the way you sleep.

It happens at regular intervals during the night, the brain shifts to what's called the rapid eye movement also known as REM sleep. It's a strange state. The brain activity increases significantly, and it appears like people who are awake, however, REM is the most difficult phase of all to awaken someone from. The REM state is where dreams occur, which researchers believe is the reason behind the eye movement that gives it the name. However, there's a different result also. When you're in REM sleep, nearly all muscles are paralyzed. This is likely to protect against injury in the event that the body attempts to perform the dream it's dreaming about. Now it appears that this paralysis could be the true reason behind stories of bizarre nighttime experiences.

After the initial 3 minutes or less of sleep, there's typically a brief period of REM during it - we'll get up briefly several times throughout the night. Most of the time, we don't even recall this, we simply wake up for a minute or two before going back to sleep. Most of the time, this wakefulness occurs after a period in REM asleep, however, occasionally the brain's control mechanisms fail. Usually , the paralysis of muscles ends after the REM happens, but sometimes it isn't. It's the result that you awake - only to realize that you're unable to move.

Sleep paralysis can be accompanied by frightening and vivid hallucinations.

Think about the scenario. It's early in the morning, and your bedroom is dim. You've just awoken from a vivid night. Your brain is at a point of transitioning between dreaming and reality. Then, suddenly you realize you're totally without a choice. Your body doesn't respond to instructions. Perhaps the most frustrating thing is that the partial paralysis of the chest muscles makes it difficult to breathe. Confounded and scared you attempt to understand everything and your mind seeks out the simplest solution it comes across There's something in there and it's on your chest.

Chapter 5: Chupacabra

Few cryptids have captured American imagination quite like the chupacabra, now a legend - or have been able to establish themselves in the popular culture so swiftly. The first mentions of the creature's existence are from 1995, and there's no previous reports of it. However, it's now an extremely well-known part in the cryptozoological bestiary with a myriad of theories about the nature of it and three distinct versions of what it appears like.

The roots of the chupacabra legend are within Puerto Rico. The legend is often said that this creature was sighted in the island for a long time but this isn't the reality. There are even claims of sightings during the 1970s are untrue according to paranormal investigator Benjamin Radford. The reality is that the myth was born in the month of March 1995 after the news media of Puerto Rico, then the global media, began reporting reports of strange deaths in livestock , mostly goats and sheep. The reports claimed that the deceased animals had strange holes in their chests, or in their throats and were completely depleted of blood. There was initially no indication of what animal was responsible for the attacks, and speculation ran rampant for a time. In November 1995, a shocking eyewitness account surfaced.

Puerto Rican woman Madelyne Tolentino claimed that she had seen the creature behind the attacks, and that it was unlike anything else on Earth. Tolentino resided in the village of Canovanas which was a recent famine of animal deaths. Up to 150 domestic and pet animals were killed and many of them displayed unusually punctured necks or chest. There were some who reported seeing strange creatures, usually flying. Then Tolentino spoke up and said she had a glimpse of the creature. The specifics of the incident aren't precise; one of the most intense accounts states that it broke into her home, tore an stuffed animal to pieces, and then fled and left behind a pool of slime as well as a piece of rancid flesh. What ever happened she described an amazing-looking creature that was unlike anything previously known to scientists. It was about three or four feet tall she claimed, sporting the gray skin of a reptile. The spines of a large row were strewn across its back, and there was no tail. It was seated on huge hind legs that were muscular and had three toed feet. It also had significantly smaller front limbs. The human-shaped head featured nostrils that were not there and large, black eyes that swung around both sides. It was the most amazing thing about it. was upright and moved about by running like the kangaroo.

A picture of the chupacabra is based on the original description of Tolentino.

When Tolentino had spoken about her encounter with the creature, it wasn't long before additional witnesses started describing something like it. More details emerged, too. There were reports that it could fly, despite not having visible wings. Others said more realistically, that it utilized its strong back legs to leap over great distances. Tolentino claimed that the eyes were black , however there was also a claim that they were red. The animal let out the sound of a terrifying sound when it was scared. It was frequently claimed that it released a scent that was sulfur-based on the ground.

It also got its own name. Due to its savage way of executing the attack, and since goats were its majority of victims people from Puerto Rico started calling it el chupacabras which is Spanish meaning "the the goat suckers".

Within weeks of the animal's existence being revealed, news began to be reported. There were reports of strange animal deaths in the neighboring countries, including that is, Dominican Republic, Colombia, Nicaragua and many more. In the places where the animal was spotted, it's appearance was generally comparable with those of Puerto Rican one. In 1996, however, the Chupacabras began moving to Mexico in the south of the USA. Then things started to alter.

The reports from Mexico as well as the USA reported the same design of deceased animals that were drained of blood, often having suspicious puncture marks however, when the predator was observed, there were significant distinctions. The powerful and upright body hind legs were gone along with the spines and the eyes that appeared alien. Witnesses described an animal that resembled the hairless coyote but with blue-gray skin, and often scaly, massive fangs and claws. They often claimed that it had a sour smell. It was not the only difference. While the creatures - sporting the name now changed to chupacabra were being reported across the USA the most popular place of sighting was Texas. Texans as well as the Mexican neighbors were both alarmed by reports of chupacabras in the area and they definitely weren't afraid to blast at the creatures. There was no time before bodies appeared to support the myth, then soon after, scientists began to consider if they had discovered a reason for the sightings.

Whatever it was, it wasn't supernatural in origin The bullets that killed them were quick enough. There is no way to know the number of victims who were shot, later tossed into the ditch, dumped or burned, but there were enough homeowners and ranchers contacted animal control to ensure a large range of bodies were readily available for inspection. The animals at first glance appeared a bit odd - human-like, yet with the thick, often scaly, skin that was gray with a distinctive blueish tint. To experts in wildlife who have experience with wild dogs and coyotes, they looked oddly shaped with large back legs and huge claws. They certainly were dogs, but they were not all the scientists that examined them was unsure about this. Next was testing DNA and shortly after the results were back. It was discovered that the North American "chupacabras" were coyotes.

These weren't normal coyotes however they appear to be suffering from Sarcoptic Mange. This is a skin condition that is caused from a small mite called Sarcoptes scabei. The mite comes in a variety of varieties and can affect a variety of species, including humans, and is very dangerous. If an infestation isn't treated, the mites will breed and expand, creating tiny holes in the skin, and then creating eggs as they move. It's extremely irritating and sufferers often scratch with a ferocious. In humans , serious cases could result in scarring. In animals with fur, the mites slowly consume hair's roots and it falls off, and the skin becomes thicker and can turn slippery. The skin also develops blue-ish hue. Mange precisely explained why the animals appeared hairless and blue. Also, it helped in explaining the reason they appeared to be oddly-shaped. We're familiar with seeing dogs and coyotes sporting their fur in good condition however, if you remove it, the body beneath is completely different shape than what we would expect. This is why the legs on the back of the animals affected appeared more long and appeared to have a distinct line along their spine. They were actually typical in shape (although typically, they were more slender) but people weren't familiar with seeing the appearance fully.

A biologist named Barry O'Connor pointed out that mange infection could also be the reason why the affected animals been attacking livestock rather than their usual prey, as the disease had made them weaker. Mange was also responsible for the stench that people who came across these animals or even killed their carcasses, complained of that the damage done by the mites provides an ideal opening for bacteria, which is why coyotes with mange often have damaged and inflamed skin.

Mange-related hair loss may cause dogs and coyotes to appear an odd appearance. Image created by Wilson Hui and used under CC by 2.0 License

It's clear that there's a reason for the four-legged chupacabras that are found throughout Mexico as well as the USA however, what is the first animal that spawned the myth? The animal Madelyne

Tolentino described was certainly not a slender dog, but its distinctive appearance of an alien. Benjamin Radford, intrigued at the report and intrigued by the story, decided to visit Puerto Rico investigating it and focused on the description of Tolentino. It was clear her animal that she drawn was not a resemblance to any species found within Puerto Rico, so there was no evidence to be found in the island. To get to the truth of the matter, Radford conducted all interviews with Tolentino that he could track down and found a bit of information that other investigator had either overlooked or didn't realize the importance of. After rechecking the details and concluding that he'd found the answer to the mystery of the Chupacabra.

The creature Tolentino had described was not a Puerto Rican animal. It was in fact an extraterrestrial. But it wasn't a genuine one.

On July 7th, 1995 - a little just one month after Tolentino's appearance - a horror science fiction film was released on Puerto Rican theaters. The film was titled Species which was about a group of scientists who were trying to locate a deadly human/alien hybrid called Sil before she was able to marry human males and form the new monster race. The creature was humanoid in form that was which was played by Natasha Henstridge, but could change into a more terrifying shape. It was smaller and was able to walk on hind legs as a kangaroo, and could form tentacles or spines on its back. It actually had an uncanny resemblance Chupacabra Tolentino reported seeing. Also, Radford believes he understands the reason.

in 1997 Scott Corrales, a prominent author of works about cryptozoology Ufology as well as the paranormal was interviewed by Tolentino for one of the chapters of Chupacabras and Other Mysteries. According to Corrales wrote in the book, the primary witness identified connections to Sil And the Chupacabra:

'(Sil) was an animal that resembled the chupacabra with spines hanging from its rear, and everything else. ....The similarities to the chupacabra is remarkable. ....I watched the film and was struck by the thought of 'My God! How could they create such a film, considering the current situation on the streets of Puerto Rico?"'

The opening sequences of the film are set in the Arecibo Observatory in Puerto Rico.

Radford realized that this was proof to Tolentino that the film was based on actual circumstances, which were happening on the island of Puerto Rico at the time she saw it. her own remarks to Corrales are in favor of this notion. What is Radford correct? Did the first sightings of chupacabras come from the inexplicably vivid imagination of an eyewitness who was under the influence of striking images of a science fiction horror film?

It's hard to say for certain however, the evidence suggests Radford's opinion is the right one. Tolentino cannot be considered an impartial witness because she has admitted that, according to her own words she felt that the film had an impact on her. Of course , there's an unquestionable fact that animal were mysteriously killed throughout Puerto Rico and elsewhere, however the recent chupacabra phenomena that has been sweeping across Mexico as well as the USA provides the evidence to that question - that the culprits are likely coyotes or wild dogs some of which could be affected by mange. There's a good chance that something else exists, but as of the moment there's nothing to prove it however all we can do to be certain is that the story of the chupacabra may represent a dog that has shaggy fur tale.

Chapter 6: Deadly Worms

Everyone has played with earthworms the time of their lives regardless of whether parents are likely to be averse - and the slim, slimy creatures are loved by gardeners because of the way they mix with and help to aerate the soil. The biologist Charles Darwin himself once said, "It may be doubted whether there are any other animals that have played as significant a part in the development of this planet such as these poorly organized creatures." It's likely to be the case; the positive effects of wormsthat are able to break down dead plants, and disperse them across the soil, as well as creating air in their networks of tunnels are crucial for farmers. Worms also serve as a significant source of food for moles, birds as well as other species of animals. They also annoy the sensitive. they're merely helpful, harmless creatures. How could a legend worm end up being considered to be one of the more terrorized creatures throughout South America, and why is it believed to be terrorizing Steppes in Mongolia?

The myth of the legend of Minhocao is traced to the Mayan civilization, which flourished throughout South as well as Central America from about 2,600 BC until the arrival of the Spanish in the 16th century. Later on in their history, the Mayans constructed elaborate temples, archaeologists are also able to find drawings and cave artifacts dating back to the beginning of their civilization. Some depict an amazing creature. At first glance , it appears like a massive snake however, a closer inspection suggests that it could be a huge worm. Of course, Mayan mythology had many bizarre creatures, so this one was not taken seriously. However, at the beginning of the 19th century, the perception of Mayan mythology began to shift.

In 1816, a French botanist from France, Augustin Saint-Hilaire, travelled to Brazil and started an expedition to the jungles and mountains that surrounded the inside. This was among the most significant biological achievements of the 20th century. Saint-Hilaire gathered tens of thousands of specimens, including over 24,000 plants from 6,000 species as well as thousands of birds, 16,000 insect species and a myriad of reptiles, fish and mammals. Many of these were species that had not been found prior to this and the Frenchman would spend the majority of the remainder of his life writing down the things he discovered. The scientist didn't only collect specimens, the Frenchman also wrote stories. When he was a young man, about around two hundred years ago, the lines between cryptozoology and zoology was much less clear as it is now, and scientists were more open to fanciful stories from indigenous peoples. A few of the stories told by Saint-Hilaire were of the existence of a huge worm in the pools and swamps or was lurking in fords along the region's numerous rivers. There was a time when it was believed that the beast - hundreds of yards long and black, with two tentacles on its head would capture livestock from fords and riverbanks , and then drag the animals in a struggle into a watery tomb. The locals referred to it as the Minhocao according to Saint-Hilaire that it was a name he believed was derived from the Portuguese term for earthworms - minhoca.

In 1877, a different European science researcher German Zoologist Fritz Muller wrote an article in an German magazine , which addressed the creature. The work of Muller was then published in the renowned British scientific journal Nature and from there the media was able to pick it up in a brief period of time. Brazil's famous giant worm was popular as well as the humorous magazine Punch featured the creature (with it being suggested that any bored of beef should consider eating the worm). Muller's story contained plenty of fresh information however. The Minhocao could be up to fifty yards long and five feet wide Some witnesses said that it had a snout resembling the snout of a pig. Locals were able to show Muller trenches, which they claimed were made from the animals' dungeons, some of them were located near swamps. The trenches could be 10 feet or more wide. Eyewitness accounts - of that Muller has collected numerous of were blamed on the Minhocao for tearing down trees or damaging the ponds that they relied upon for water sources.

Eyewitness accounts suggest that the Minhocao has distinct tentacles that hang from its head.

Rumors of similar animals have also were reported from different South American countries and European researchers were quick to investigate. They couldn't always locate anything, but they did find. One tourist in Nicaragua approached an official in the area who'd worked on the island for 12 many years, about gigantic worms. the official said they'd never heard of anything like it. But some people did hear stories of the creatures, and scientists have also found previous references to the creature.

Zoologists of the present are skeptical of the existence the Minhocao particularly since sightings of the animal appear to have waned and there's been few eyewitness accounts in more than 100 years. It's not impossible to believe that the Minhocao is actually present however, as there are other known - and smaller creatures that have many similarities to the Minhocao. While the Minhocao is commonly referred to as the worm, it has some specific characteristics that have been reported by people who saw it - such as the pig's snout and, sometimes, teeth that are large that sound more similar to a vertebrate. The scaly skin some people have reported doesn't quite seem to fit with the idea of the idea that this animal is an animal. However, there's another possibility, and it's intriguing enough on its own.

Caecilians are amphibians, which is the same animal species like frogs, toads, and newts.

They don't resemble whatsoever to frogs but. Instead, the diverse species ranging between a few inches and almost five feet in length are more like snakes or worms with their slim, long bodies but without legs. The way they behave is also unique. A majority of amphibians reside in or near water, but caecilians can be described as burrowers. They have sturdy skulls, pointed snouts. They also have muscles to push their way through the soil. They accomplish this by expanding the muscles to the back of their bodies to secure themselves in their burrows, then pushing their head into the ground towards the front. They also can take a dip in water or soft mud. Although most caecilians are breathing lungs, there are two species that don't however, they are able to be able to absorb oxygen from their skins which allows to breathe deep underground. The eyes of caecilians are tiny and, in order to guard them in the burrows of animals they are protected by their skin, and are almost invisibly invisible. the majority of species of caecilians aren't blind, as people think however their vision is only able to tell whether it's dark or light. They don't appear above the surface in daylight because they are prone to being hunted by predators, therefore being capable of determining whether the sun is still out is essential for them. However, in general they don't have to be able to see even though zoologists don't understand all that much about them as they would like to believe, it appears they are mostly eating termites and worms. They are able to hunt down by using their other senses which are extremely sensitive. Researchers believe that caecilians are adept at detecting vibrations, similar to other species of the underground, and several species also possess a pair of tentacles on their head that are believed to be connected with their smell sense. In addition, the tentacles look like miniature versions of the ones that many witnesses have described on the head of Minhocao.

Caecilians aren't big, but their appearance is very similar to the Minhocao. Image taken by Dick Culbert and used under CC by 2.0 License

Is it possible that a huge caecilian dwells beneath that soil in Brazilian forests, but occasionally come up to the surface to terrorize locals and create havoc by digging huge burrows? Yes, it's possible. The biological reason is as to why earthworms can't reach the size of a giant. Certain worms can grow to great lengths. For instance, one marine nematode known as known as the bootlaceworm (Lineus longissimus) can reach up to 180 feet. It's just less than one-quarter of an inch in circumference however, as the worm becomes bigger than it is, its skin must be so thick that it wouldn't breathe through the pores. The same limitation doesn't apply to caecilians. Since it's a vertebrate, the skeleton is there that can support its body weight. it doesn't require a thick skin to support itself. It also has lungs and it can breath through the mouth. It's possible that's the reason why the Minhocao digs a hole close to the surface and appears to be above ground it could require such a large amount of oxygen that it's unable to stay alive on the stuff that's within the earth.

It's not likely that the Minhocao will attain the size described in some articles - over a hundred foot in length - but there's a any reason why a caecilian could not become as big as a snake. It's a bit shocking that a creature this huge hadn't yet been found by scientists before but keep in mind the enormous goblin shark and squid which are also huge creatures that were discovered just recently. They are found in deep ocean, making them difficult to locate However, one that lived the majority of its existence underground in forests that are remote could be hard to find also.

As captivating as it may be but it is, Minhocao isn't the only worm that's intriguing. Minhocao can't be the only scary creature that's believed to exist. On the other end of the planet is a different and more terrifying creature that was rumored by the natives of in the Gobi desert for centuries, but was not known to the West until 1926. The olgoi-khorkhoi is more commonly referred to as the Mongolian death worm.

It is believed that the Mongolian Death Worm is smaller than Minhocao with some witnesses describing it to be between two to five feet in length. It's a lot more pervasively hazardous, though. Sausage-shaped, and ominous blood red hue It's believed to have numerous methods to kill or kill its adversaries. It is able to spray acidic venom which kills human beings upon contact. It can also damage metals and also emit lethal electric shocks. Contact with it can cause extreme discomfort, but more often the outcome is immediate death. The worm burrows into the sand and creates visible waves on the surface , which reveal its dark presence. According to locals, they were attracted by the yellow hue and was known eating plants specifically goyo, a parasitic plant.

The death worm has never ever been mentioned in the west prior to American naturalist Roy Chapman Andrews, often believed to be the person who inspired Indiana Jones, traveled through Mongolia in four separate expeditions between 1922 to 1925. When he attended a conference with an official group from the local government, they were informed of the worm. Even though the worm was a mystery to him personally that none of the people who he met had experienced it personally, even though they all believed in its existence the worm was mentioned in his 1926 novel On The Trail of Ancient Man. The creature received a brief appearance in the book, however it ignited the interest of a lot of cryptozoologists, and that fascination has never waned.

Despite the excitement that the death worm sparked, however, it took years before anyone went to find it. Then Czech investigator of paranormal activity Ivan Mackerle, who had previously searched in search of Loch Ness Monsters, Loch Ness Monster began an investigation to locate this death worm. Two visits in the years 1990 and 1992 yielded sufficient material and local accounts to create a television documentary, but there was no physical evidence. After a gap that lasted more than a decade the researcher conducted a second investigation in 2004. Mackerle employed innovative methods to track down the worm by smuggling explosives into Mongolia through the Russian frontier and blasting them into areas likely to be affected and the shock waves the theory goes, will drive the worm towards the surface in order to avoid the concussion. The plan didn't work and the extensive footage filmed by an ultralight plane in 2004 did not show any indication of the waves that the creature was supposed to generate. Mackerle also discovered that death worm could be an illusion, caused through stress and the extreme heat of the Gobi Desert.

So , is Mackerle accurate or is it possible that this Mongolian death worm really be an actual animal? It's not easy to determine. There are some issues with the tale. Worms like moist environments as is the case in they are attracted to moist conditions. Gobi Desert can be as dry as you can possibly obtain - the average rainfall across its vast area is just less than 8 inches per year. And even that figure is altered due to the monsoons which reach the southeast corner. The rest is much dryer. It's difficult to think of a creature like a worm able to live in cold deserted Sands.

Does the creature really exist as a parasite, or is it a worm? The rumored ability of the creature to release electricity isn't as impressive as it sounds. Electric eels, which are one of the species of knifefish can unleash a massive 860 volt charge on its prey. Torpedo rays produce smaller voltage, but significantly higher current, and similarly devastating consequences for its victim. While the claims of it killing at a distance by generating electricity are unbelievable, the idea that someone who touches it could be hit with a fatal shock is totally plausible.

The electric eel is able to stun or kill prey with a an electric shock of high voltage. Image created by Chrisbb and licensed under the CC 2.0. 2.0 License

It is also possible that the creature actually a snake, which is why it is able to spray the venom. Spitting cobras and vipers hunt their victims, just like other snakes with venom infusing them with poison using their hollow fangs. However in the event of danger, they may employ an alternative way to defend themselves. the openings in the fangs which release the venom are smaller and point straight forwards, and by contracting the muscles surrounding the venom sacs, they are able to discharge a spray of venom up to the distance of six feet. Cobra venom is safe when it hits intact human skin. It isn't harmful, but the fundamental principle is the same and when it gets into the eyes of the victim, it can cause severe pain and sometimes blindness. When the target is blinded, the cobra could then use the chance to strike with an extremely fatal bite.

The Mongolian disease isn't totally impossible, but at the moment there's no evidence that there's a real possibility. What's the likelihood? There's no way to know. Gobi is a vast area with more than half a million square miles but is inhabited by a few nomads. There's plenty of space for animals to hide under the ground without being noticed by scientists. Much like the Minhocao it's a hypnoticly plausible cryptid, even if certain details are embellished or invented.

Chapter 7: Megaconda

Giant worms are firmly in cryptid territory. However, giant snakes are a fact. There are many snakes that can develop into large size and the most deadly one, the inland taipan can reach up to eleven feet but the most massive and heavy are the constrictors. They are able to kill prey by wrapping around their bodies and compressing the ribcage in order to stop it breathing. The longest snake on the planet is a constrictor, called the Reticular Python, which is able to increase to 23 feet long and perhaps even 30 feet however, pythons are comparatively slim snakes. They're not the same as of South America's counterpart snake, the anaconda.

The green anaconda is among the largest snake ever found. It's smaller than the large Python (the longest known specimen measured 19.4 feet) however the muscular body of its is larger and more robust. An anaconda weighs 50 percent more than a snake with the same size. It may not have the same amount of distance from between the tail and the nose, however it's a formidable snake. Despite the fact that they've never been linked to an individual's death - as opposed to snakes that have killed and likely consumed people in the wild as well as in captive - there's no doubt that if an anaconda was wrapped around a person, they'd encounter a lot of difficulty being able to survive the event. Their prey of choice is nearly everything they can capture and kill, such as deer, tapirs, fish as well as small crocodiles. It is a powerful swimmer, and lives the majority of its time in or in water. One of its many names local to it is water boa. They typically snare prey with their paws by lying in the water with just their noses visible above the surface. When a predator is close enough, the anaconda can attack quickly and swiftly and firmly encase the victim's body before closing the animal to death before eating it. It usually hunts at night So the chances of spotting the snake before it strikes are low.

The green anaconda is an extremely stunning snake, and certainly should not be tripped over in the slightest in its natural surroundings. It would seem like enough to make it a part of the story in mythology and for zoologists they are. For cryptozoologists, however there are intriguing rumors of a larger snake that lurks in the moist deeps of South America's rain forests. These rumors actually have been around for a long time. When Europeans first began to explore the rainforests, they brought back stories of anacondas weighing 150 feet or more capable of crushing small vessels or eating a whole portions of explorers as small as the size of a handful of peanuts.

The anaconda's size is impressive, but it is elusive. Image created by Ivan Mlinaric and used under CC by 2.0 License

As researchers learned more about the anaconda, reports of the amount of snake started to shrink, as often is the case in these situations. In the early 20th century, 30 feet was thought to be an accurate size, though stories of larger ones still came up often. A few of them appear to be credible, but they are not backed by tangible evidence such as bones. It is nevertheless accepted that anacondas that are greater than of 30 feet are living active in the depths of the jungle. The evidence to support this is an observation that constrictors of this are that large were certainly present in the past. Titanoboa cerrejonensis was found in the area that is today South America 60 million years ago, is believed to be at most 42 feet as well as weigh more than a ton. It's nearly twice what the size of biggest known anaconda, with eight-times the mass. While the climate was more warm at the time, which allowed reptiles and snakes to expand there's no reason that anacondas of this size wouldn't be able to survive in the tropical regions of today. Since larger snakes are able to save heat more effectively, it's feasible that the colder climate will allow them to grow even larger sizes. Scientists have suggested that the main aspect on animals such as Titanboa was the extent to which they could grow without overheating.

The majority of accounts of enormous anacondas don't have any credibility Eyewitness accounts are often wildly wild because it's difficult to gauge the size of a snake , especially when it's in a coiled state. If you've actually caught one it's incredibly difficult to determine the size, but. Constrictors of enormous size are extremely strong and difficult to separate. To manage them properly, the rule of thumb for zookeepers is two people for a three-foot snake and another for each three feet in length. An anaconda that is 30 feet long would require eleven people to secure it.

Even then, its massive body would be in constant movement, writhing and stretching as it tried to escape. Under those circumstances, it's not simple to obtain a reliable measurement, and the experience suggests that any measurement taken from a conscious constrictor may be off by more than 30% in any direction. To straighten them and determine their length implies that the snake is been killed, or at the very least, tranquilized. The majority of assertions of massive anacondas are not supported by evidence. It's easy to say that you killed an enormous snake in the forest however without the skull, there's no way to prove the fact.

Certain accounts are more trustworthy than others, however. Col. Percy Fawcett was one of the most well-known British explorationists in the 20th century's early years A gunnery expert, he mixed his military work with trips to Ceylon (now Sri Lanka) and later South America. In 1906, Fawcett was commissioned to the Royal Geographical Society to survey the frontier that separated Brazil and Bolivia and, in September of that year was an English engineer by the name of Arthur Chivers and twenty locally recruited men set out in the forest. It was a gruelling hike. Chivers fell sick with fever and had to be evacuated back to civilization, along with an unspecified group of sick people. Chivers was among the fortunate ones. Fawcett was one of the Jamaican known as Willis along with a dozen other men continued their march across the border that was disputed. After eight months of setting off, three of them were rescued from the green hell. All the others were dead. Fawcett, however, had successfully surveyed and traced the boundary and returned with a wealth of stories from the jungle. One was about a gigantic snake.

According to Fawcett , his expedition was drifting along to the Rio Abuna, a tributary of the Amazon and the head of a massive anaconda suddenly emerged from the water , a few feet away off the bow of the boat. Fawcett picked up his gun and fired, firing the snake through its spine, a couple of feet below the head. The water turned into foam when it crashed briefly and its body hit the hull before it sank to the bottom. The explorers carried the corpse to shore, then stretched it out and arrived at an amazing number. "As as could be measured the length, 45 feet was visible from the water, and 17 feet were on the bottom of the sea, giving the total length 62 feet" according to Fawcett "Its the body wasn't particularly large it was not more than 12 inches in size However, it was likely to have been long and hungry." It was more than double the length that anacondas were believed to be in the past and the response to Fawcett's story in the scientific and western media was mocking.

However, should the account of Fawcett be erased as quickly like it did in 1907? Most likely not. Fawcett was a unique person who later in his life, was fascinated by the concept of a lost city in the Amazon and in 1925, Fawcett disappeared together as his child Jack and a young man, in the process of searching for the city. He had also been a very meticulous individual who was a highly-trained artillery officer who also completed the Royal Geographical Society's highly regarded training for explorationists. Both elements of his education were geared towards accuracy and truthful reporting. Also, he had been a licensed surveyor who was adept in judging distances. His integrity and honesty was unquestioned and in 1916, he nearly was arrested Winston Churchill on suspicion of being a German spy. It's possible that Fawcett was wrong on the length of the snake he shot however it's highly unlikely that to believe he was lying about it and even if he was off by 20 feet, it's more than any previously documented.

There's absolutely no biological reason for why anacondas of this size shouldn't exist as well as the Amazon basin of 2.2 million sq miles of impenetrable rainforest, and dotted with numerous rivers could be the perfect environment for the animals. Humans have already visited the vast majority of it, areas , they remain virtually uninhabited and in fact, today many excursions into these regions just disappear. The most modern training and equipment are not enough to compete with the wild and its inhabitants. Are massive anacondas, 60 feet in length, or even bigger, in the ranks of those inhabitants? Yes, it's possible.

Chapter 8: Orang-Bati

Humanoid cryptids are not new. Indeed, many of the most well-known unknown creatures belong to this category, like Bigfoot along with The Himalayan Yeti. They're usually quite like Bigfoot as they are both large hairy human beings who are found in woods - and according to the people who study them, they're considered to be shy and quiet. There are exceptions however and one is thought to be quite hazardous. It's the Orang-bati mystery cryptid with a peculiar cryptid said to be haunting on the Indonesian Island of Seram.

When people first are introduced to the term "Orang-bati", they are struck by the similarities in resemblance to Orangutan, the great ape. it's not surprising since both names have the same linguistic roots. Orangutan refers to "forest or "forest-loving person" from Malay and Indonesian from the words "orang" (person) or "hutan" (forest). Orang-bati is a similar word, translating to "winged individual".

It's true that the Orang-bati is a humanoid that fly. Locals living on Seram the biggest island in the Indonesian Maluku Province, describe it as a tiger-like creature which is about 5 feet tall. It has the reddish color of its fur as well as a lengthy thin tail, and massively extended arms that support a pair of bat-like, leathery wings. At first glance , it appears like flying monkeys from The Wizard of Oz, but this is actually a far more terrifying creature. The inhabitants of Seram believe that there is a community of Orang-Bati that live in caves in Mount Kairatu, an extinct volcano that lies in the middle on the Island. In these caves, the creatures appear at night, and they attack villages around them.

The Orang-bati from Seram legend is believed to be a predator. People in the region say that flying creatures roam the skies around villages and emit a crying sound, while they search for their preferred prey, children. When children are spotted, the creature comes down to attack the victim, taking it hostage and transporting it back to caves, where it will be eaten.

However terrifying it might be an animal, the Orang-bati isn't well recognized within the western world. It has a long-standing history on Seram but. The first non-natives to learn about Seram were Christian missionaries during the early 16th century, however these stories were largely dismissed as untrue. They were repeated in the course of time, every generation. As technology advanced, westerners stopped listening , and the little information about the creature that lived outside Indonesia was lost but fascinating stories don't be forgotten forever, which is why this story was going to be no exception.

In 1987, an English Missionary named Tyson Hughes traveled to Seram to help locals construct stronger farms. While there, he heard stories from the people of the Seram region whom he worked with. Being a shrewd Anglican Hughes was very skeptical of any supernatural phenomenon however he did take notes of the stories and publish them after returning from his trip. Most likely, the response was more skeptical However, some people found the story about the monkey flying fascinating and began to associate the tale with other stories in the same region.

In reality, there were efforts to connect the Orang-bati with other creatures all over the world such as that of the American "batsquatch" reported to have been observed close to Mt. Saint Helens in 1994. Batsquatch isn't considered a serious threat by the majority of cryptozoologists. Attention has been focused at Asian and Pacific countries with their unique fly-like humanoid cryptozoids. There are several of them. On Java For instance - an additional Indonesian island - is the chimp-like Ahool that is believed to have wingspans of as long as 12 feet. The Ahool typically eats fish according to witnesses, however attacks on humans are speculated to be happening too. It's also known as the Ropen that is believed to reside inside Indonesia's Papua province as well as an island in Papua New Guinea. There are some who claim that the Ropen appears similar to a reptile extinct flying reptile however there are some who've claimed it's more like flying monkeys. However, all of them are well-known across Indonesia and have a similar role in the local mythology of cryptozoology, similar in the same way as Bigfoot and Bigfoot in the USA or the Loch Ness Monster in Scotland. Naturally, once researchers began to connect the various animals and the Loch Ness Monster, speculation began to rise on the possible reasons for the similar stories.

One of the first things that need to be mentioned is that according to zoologists, there isn't a concept as a flying monkey. The flying mammal is a fact definitely - indeed, five percent of mammals can fly, making them a bigger group than all other species, with the exception of rodents. There are many others that are able to glide but none are monkeys. The closest ones are colugos that is flying lemurs. They're not monkeys, but are primates and belong to the same family as humans and monkeys. They're even found in the right area of the globe. One of two species - Sunda flying lemur is indigenous to Indonesia.

The Orang-bati isn't flying lemur, however. Colugos are around 2 feet long, including tails they weigh just 3 pounds. They're also vegetarians, surviving on leaves, flowers , and fruits. The most important thing is that they cannot fly. They have the patagium, an elastic band that connects their legs - their back and front They use it to glide across distances as long as 350 feet. Colugos live their entire existence in trees, and when they hunt, they make use of their glide to jump from tree to the trunk. It's also a great method to avoid predators that take to the trees following them. They're generally calm, gentle and peaceful creatures, but they're very different from the Orang-bati.

There's absolutely no reason why the existence of gliding monkeys is not possible patagiums have been found in many mammal groups such as squirrels and the marsupial sugar gliders in Australia There isn't any evidence to suggest that they exist or have. There aren't many monkeys that are predators of serious importance and neither are they serious predators. Baboons may hunt large animals such as the goat or small antelopes. However, they're not the norm; monkeys eat leaves and fruit and will also eat eggs, birds, and small animals when they have the opportunity. There's no prey species that hunt humans - but this doesn't mean it's impossible. In general, however biologists strongly oppose the notion of flying monkeys. There's no evidence in fossil evidence to indicate that any primate ever developed bat-like wings and it's highly unlikely that such a significant change would have occurred in a way that was not noticed. If the Orang-bati is truly flying monkey, it's certainly not something that naturally evolved.

It's also possible that the Orang-bati might be an animal which resembles an animal to make it difficult for a person who isn't an expert to see, which leads us back to flying mammals. Of course, these are bats. Bats belong to the family Chiroptera that with around 1,240 species, makes them more diversifiable that any other species other than rodents (2,277 species) and are found all over across the globe, except for that of the Antarctic and the most northern regions. Bats are divided into two distinct groups. The majority of them belong to the category that most people are familiar with: the small and highly-specialized microbats that rely on echolocation to hunt for insects. There are more daring predators too; the most well-known are the tiny but well-known vampire bats that consume blood. Three species capture fish, and then snatch them from the water's surface using their clawed hind leg. The species that hunts for frogs by using its sensitive ears to locate its mating call. Greater noctule bat found in Europe, North Africa and west Asia hunts birds from the air. Two species that are the American bat spectral and the Australian ghost bat prey upon other bats.

Fruit bats are among the biggest flying mammal. Image provided by USFWS and is licensed under the CC by 2.0 License

Microbats are tiny but the largest having wingspans of approximately 18 inches, and a body just 4 inches long. It's impossible for a creature however fierce hunter it is, can be confused with flying monkeys. However, the other family of bats is quite different. Some megabats are massive - for instance, the smallest of them is barely two inches in length - but some have wingspan that is close to 6 feet. This is still a lot smaller than the size claimed by the Orang-bati, but it's a much closer than a microbat could be.

There's one major problem with the notion of the Orang-bati being considered a megabat. The most common term used to refer to megabats as fruit bats because they eat fruit. Megabats aren't the only species known to exist. is a carnivore perhaps even an insectivore. even though their teeth are often terrifying, they're all purely vegetatian. Some cryptozoologists think that the Orang-bati might in fact be remnants of a of Pterosaurs. The animals are thought to have gone extinct together with dinosaurs about 65 million years back, but they did possess features that are similar to Orang-bati, the Ropen and other cryptids similar to them. These animals had wings that resembled bats as well as fur-covered bodies. They were carnivores. In particular, some species expanded to enormous sizes, far bigger than modern bats or bird. For instance, the largest known pterosaurs possessed a wingspan of 36 feet, and an eight-foot skull. This is a lot bigger than the one the indigenous people of Seram refer to, which is at about 5 feet tall when it's lying on the ground. The animal that is similar to Moganopterus could be about the correct size it is believed to have been a part of what is today the eastern part of Asia. If the descendants of its ancestors survive within the underground caves at Mount Kairatu they would be well-equipped to take the child.

Pterosaurs can grow to impressive size. Image taken by Jim Linwood and used under CC by 2.0 License

The last possible scenario is that Orangbati is a mythical creature, a product of confusion as to what's really happening. The inhabitants of Seram have a good understanding of the fruit bats but they tend to appear larger in the night. If someone was looking in search of a lost child noticed a huge bat moving over the sky, they could easily confuse it for a huge monkey-like predator and form a link that's not really there. To determine the real nature of Orang-bati's existence, it is necessary to wait until we see an actual body or, better yet the specimen is captured.

Dingonek

The 19th century's period of exploration, Africa was often referred to by the name of "the black continent". The term is now used to make many people feel uncomfortablebecause it's not difficult to detect undertones of colonial superiority , or even racism, however, in the beginning it was a reference to the notion of Africa as an unexplored region that was full of mysteries. The animals they had observed were a bit bizarre hippos that looked placid with a violent temper and large teeth, cheetahs able to outrun even the fastest horse, or the bizarre Giraffe, and they were more likely to believe in tales of other, less spooky animals they heard about from indigenous people. A huge win for early cryptozoologists, the folklore of Africa is full of mysterious creatures, and there were plenty of stories to tell. From were-leopards, the vicious Tokoloshe to the small helpful Yumboes there's a cryptid to suit any area. The most frightening, however, are the Dingonek.

The Dingonek appears to be assembled using the spare parts of a monster creator's box. According to different accounts, it's between nine and 18 feet in length and is typically a red or gray color. The body of the beast is covered in a scaly , armored hide. Its short, strong legs are capped by reptile-like claws. The creature also has an extended tail with an elongated bone spike at its end. According local reports, it could produce a deadly venom as does scorpions' sting. The most frightening part are the heads, that is adorned with an array of sharp, long tusks that have earned it the name "jungle Walrus" from European travelers who have heard the stories.

It is believed that the legend about the Dingonek is well-known in central Africa specifically in that region in the Congo river basin (what's currently is now Democratic Republic of the Congo). This is where the majority of reports come from There are also indications - perhaps not as credible, but nevertheless fascinating - that it could be more widely spread.

The San peoples from southern Africa were once referred to as "Bushmen" and a word which is now considered offensive hunter-gatherer way of life for tens of many thousands of. Tools similar to those employed by the San are now dated to 46,000 years of age, proving their long-standing presence throughout the entire region. Additionally, they possess a long oral culture that has been handed across generations (their complex language does not have an alphabet and writing isn't a part of the culture in the traditional San cultural practices) and a history that has been based on cave paintings. For centuries , at the very least, they San have been creating art on cave walls and stones by mixing animal fats and colored powdered rocks. Since fats are used to binder the drawings can withstand the elements of rain and wind for long before they fade away, but when they're kept in caves, they'll endure for centuries. What's unique with San painting is the fact that even though they're stylized, their portrayal of animals - which is the primary motif - is more real than the majority of paintings made in caves. A large part of this is due to their ability to paint using a tiny animal-hair brushes or just a tiny feather, which allows fine details to be captured as well as the rest from their extensive experience with the creatures they hunt or play with. One San painting appears to depict something similar to those in the Congolese description of Dingonek.

There's some debate regarding the painting. Although it's readily available online, it's often claimed to have been discovered in "Brackfontein Ridge" in South Africa. However, there's no place like that. But if the spelling of the word is changed to match the Afrikaans conventions and is renamed "Brakfontein" There's an unincorporated town with this name located in the Eastern Cape province. Brakfontein is situated in the middle of mountains which is exactly the kind of location that the San like to paint in their paintings. The image is stunningly clear, and some might think that it's suspicious. However, it does depict a variety of animals. Three can be identified as wildebeest as well as a porcupine and Jackal, however the two others are more elusive. In the background , there is what could be a huge snake with horns - another cryptid , or perhaps a duiker that is heavily stylized. The one in the foreground, is a representation of the evidence of the Dingonek all the way to the walrus ' tusks.

The animal depicted in the lower left corner of the cave painting is very similar to description of Dingonek.

It's very likely that this photo is fake. In the photos online of it the surface appears to be flawless and clean It could be the result of a piece of paper that has been painted to mimic the look of rocks. It's also hard to find any academic reference to this, suggesting that it may have been made by a cryptid enthusiast who was overly enthusiastic. If the original can be located and authenticated it would provide convincing evidence of that the Dingonek exists. Dingonek. The San do not often depict fictional creatures in their artwork. They do draw fantastical creatures, but they are San men wearing animal heads and are the traditional healers of the tribe.

In addition to in addition to "Brakfontein" artwork and other accounts from Congolese indigenous people, there's more evidence of the Dingonek as well. At the very least, one

European explorationist claimed to have witnessed, and even killed, the Dingonek. John Alfred Jordan, a nomad who was a farmer, prospector, as well as a variety of other occupations, but always ended being a hunter and surveyor in Africa He led an expedition to the Kenyan Migori River in 1907. One day his Lumbwa Scouts had been sent forward, returned later to report there was a bizarre creature floating in the river far from where they were. Jordan was able to move along the river, with his rifle at ready, and rounded around to find an enormous 15-foot beast within the stream , less than ten feet away. He sat in awe for a couple of minutes, but, fearing the animal would come back and look at him, he raised his .303 Lee-Enfield rifle , and fired it directly behind the ear. A .303 shot in the head can knock down a rhino however, the Dingonek simply jumped into the air, spinning rapidly toward the explorer who was gone. When Jordan noticed that the bullet didn't kill immediately, he ran to the bush and concealed.

A creature as large as the Dingonek alive and extinct been recognized as a living thing and Africa is not an unexplored continent anymore. There are still huge, nearly inaccessible rain forests and a large animal could be able to hide in the forest and rivers. The Dingonek is said to be fiercely protective and may kill crocodiles, hunters and even hippos when they wander too close to their nest. If it's able to be able to withstand a shot to the head by a powerful caliber bullet, it's unlikely anyone who has stumbled across an animal in wild will come back to tell the story. It's true that it's unlikely that such a bizarre and dangerous creature really does exist, it's hard to be certain.

Elwetritsch

We've examined a broad variety of cryptids within this book. The existence of a few seems highly probable. Megalodon is one example. or Akkorukamai. Both are variations of animals that are known to exist today there's no reason why the more complex, more complex cryptozoological forms aren't lurking in the depths. Other species are more unclear. There's a possibility that the orang-bati as well as Dingonek aren't like any other known animal, however there are many possibilities that make sense.

However, there are a few obscure cryptids, not all, but a handful which are easily traced by a little effort. Sometimes, the truth is far more complex than any myth could ever be. One instance of this is the legend of Elwetritsch.

It is Elwetritsch is a peculiar small, tiny creature that is believed to live in Germany's forests. Rhineland-Palatinate region. It is essentially the chicken, but is covered in scales rather than feathers and its wings are too small for flying. Certain illustrations depict it with antlers that are small and females are typically depicted as having breasts. Elwetritsch Elwetritsch is deeply ingrained in the cultural heritage that is the Palatinate and several town squares display the Elwetritsch as statues of ornamental beauty or fountains. Kaiserslautern Zoo has a display featuring figures of the animal and is a favorite topic among local social clubs.

The Elwetritsch frequently appears in Palatinate town fountains and statues.

But, the most fascinating and intriguing local custom that involves the animal has to be the Elwetritsch hunt. It is a tradition that has been followed for years about this. Elwetritsch Elwetritsch is known for being mysterious, yet is a bit curious. It is attracted by light and when it's examining the light source, it can be captured. A hunting group is comprised of the "catcher" typically the youngest person in the group, as well as several beaters. The catcher is outfitted with a sack and lantern, while beaters generally use sticks. The hunt will begin when the catcher is taken to a suitable spot in the forest. There, they can light their lanterns and then sit down with their bag. The idea is that the animal is able to escape the beaters, will become enticed by the glow and will wander across the forest to gaze at it. As it is distracted, the catcher is able to easily catch it and put it in his bag. After preparing the trap, the beaters set out for the edges of the woods. Then they'll make a line, and move back toward the catcher, directing the animal towards him , and the lantern.

That's the way they say to the catcher about what they're planning to tell him. Actually, the beaters instantly make their way to the nearest pub and have several beers before the catcher realizes that they've been tricked, and then walks from the forest to join the beaters. Since it is believed that the Elwetritsch hunt is a sly play on the new members of hunter's clubs and social clubs as well as the Elwetritsch itself is the older

German equivalent to the American Jackalope.

Certain cryptids may be raised to the status of an officially recognized species. That's been the case with the okapi, one of the relatives that of the giraffe. Prior to the beginning of the 20th century it was only known through tales told by natives and occasional glimpses of its zebra-striped back fleeing to the woods. Today, it's as a an integral part of zoology's mainstream like any animal. African animal, and there are many Okapis living in zoos all over the globe. Sometimes, cryptids are proved to be a hoax. Bear Lake Monster Bear Lake Monster was reported in and close to Bear Lake on the Utah-Idaho border since 1868. However, in 1894, it was discovered to be "a amazing first-class fabrication" by the person who had invented the legend, which included tales of the past Indian legends , to add some authenticity. But in a fascinating example of the power of myth, this Bear Lake Monster has continued to be observed regularly since, by those who probably heard the original legend but not the more recent account; the last recorded sighting was in 2002.

Chapter 9: Air

Mothman

Locality: Point Pleasant, West Virginia; Butler County, Pennsylvania; New York Twin Towers; Tower Bridge, Sacramento; (although occasional sightings have been reported throughout North America)

Description of the flying Humanoid. The creature is at around 7 feet tall. Witnesses have described massive bat-like wings, shrieking voice, and the most distinct big glowing red eyes.

If you're playing paranormal or cryptid bingo, and you've have hit the jackpot with Mothman. Mothman is a complete package:

It's not much more terrifying than the first time Mothman was seen that took place in the month of November in 1966. It occurred at Colendenin, West Virginia when five men were digging a grave when they saw the massive creature flying over the horizon.

Most accounts suggest that the creature's physical attributes look more like a humanoid flying bat or bird as opposed to those of a moth. The name was derived from a character in The Batman TV series that was very popular at the time.

Perhaps the most well-known sighting reported was on the 15th of November in 1966, when two married couples were driving by an World War II ammunitions plant that was referred to locally in the area as "TNT Zone."

The couple, Steve and Mary Mallette and Roger and Linda Scarberry, stated that the first thing that attracted their interest was big red eyes. They claimed that the creature was enchanting or hypnotic effects on the couple.

"It was the eyes that sucked us in," said Linda. "It was a big red eyes, reminiscent of reflective lenses in cars."

The couple estimated that the creature stood nearly seven feet high and describe it as a humanoid with bat-like wings large enough to be were folded over its back and sides.

Afraid of the creature The couple drove to the village in Point Pleasant, West Virginia.

Sometimes, they saw the flying beast keeping up with their car. They even believed that the beast was able to fly with speeds as high as 100 miles an hour! The beast pursued the group for seven miles then fled into the night after they got to the city's limits.

They also said that the creature produced the sound of a whirring which could be heard through the roar of the engine in the car that was like the sound of a "record playing at high speed."

In addition to proving credibility of the account They did not stop the car until they arrived at the Mason County Sheriff's Office. The four shared their incident with the deputy Millard Halstead. It was evident that no matter what they saw the four were shocked. The deputy Halstead said later, "I've known these kids for a long time. They'd never been in trouble, and they were very terrified that night."

Despite being a little agitated by the events of the night The two couples arranged to let the Deputy take them to the place where they first encountered the creature. When he arrived, his patrol vehicle produced a loud, squealing sound, which forced the Deputy

Halstead to switch off his radio. He carried out an investigation into the area but found no evidence.

The 1975 novel by John Keel, The Mothman Prophecies, not only introduced people to this truly terrifying mysterious, mysterious, and mysterious mystery, but it also gives a comprehensive list of all-star paranormal actors who also appeared in Point Pleasant West, Virginia from November 1966 until December 1967.

West Virginia has a rich tradition of being a place that is full of ghosts and bizarre creatures. Many Native American tribes would avoid going into the area altogether. Some even believe that the very appearance of Mothman to the occurrence of a Native American curse brought on by the demise of chief Cornstalk. In the wake of his own demise, made a declaration that was often translated according to the following:

"I went to your home to visit a friend, and you've killed me. You have killed my son, Ellinipisico. This is why be the curses of the Great Spirit be enshrined on this place. Could this spot be cursed in the hands of the nature? Will its hopes remain destroyed

...although White Man might conquer the Valley His insatiable ambition will cause the earth to be ruined as well as the water unusable and the air intoxicated."

It all boils to a matter of perception. Some believe Mothman is a sign of indication of imminent disaster, while others believe that Mothman is the one who causes the catastrophes that appear to revolve around his spotting spots.

Also also known as: Thunderbird

The best evidence is eyewitness testimony, including police reports.

Barred Owls

There is a reason to be skeptical Some skeptical individuals suggest that the sightings are the result of mistaken identification of barred owls, which are well-known to have a eyes with red shine.

Thunderbirds

The location is all over North America

Description: Enormous raptor. A wingspan of 15-25 feet. A large hook bill that can be called having teeth that are sharp. Talons with hooks.

In second place behind Bigfoot in the number of reported encounters Thunderbirds were seen in flight over large parts in North America for hundreds - or even thousands of years. As with many North American cryptids, Thunderbirds are strongly connected in Native American and first Nations mythologies, legends and cultures.

Certain North American indigenous people's culture and past believe they believe that Thunderbirds are their ancestral ancestors. While much differs from one culture to another but it is generally accepted that it's not a good idea to provoke the Thunderbird. Certain tribes believe that Thunderbirds have the ability to change shape into human forms and even reproduce with humans.

The Thunderbird is thought to be as a bird that is supernatural in its strength and power. They are also believed to be capable of causing storms as well as producing lightning and thunder while flying. Legend says that clouds are tangled by the wingbeats of its wings. Sheet lightning happens as the animal blinks and the lightning bolts are produced from the glow of snakes that it carries along with it during flight.

One of the most fascinating myths concerning Thunderbirds originates out of The Sioux folks who believed that Thunderbirds defeated reptile monsters known as the Unktehila.

There is a general belief that no bird of prey has the capability of flying away with children and even an adult. There is belief that certain species like those of the Golden Eagle and the African crowned Eagle (which has been observed to hunt animals that weigh as much as 65lbs!) can be large enough to cause harm to children or infants.

Golden Eagle striking an deer

There is evidence in archaeology that our planet had a population of huge birds, called gigantic teratorns, such as, Argentavis magnificens, which was the biggest flying bird ever found. With wingspans of 30 feet, a standing taller than six feet and weighing more than an average human being, these remarkable birds are reminiscent of the modern-day stories of Thunderbirds. About six million years ago, these flying wonders flew over today's Argentina.

Aiolornis incredibilis is the biggest known bird to fly that was found in North America. It was a bird that flew with an impressive 16 feet of wingspan and was in existence as recently like 10,000 years prior, that's right, it was near to humans. With its strong bill and bird-of prey on steroids appearance, it would have amazed and scared those who came across it. It is believed that the animal is extinct, could a tiny breeding population be the reason for the astonishing Thunderbird sightings?

A tragic incident with an Thunderbird is reported to have happened within Tippah County Missouri during 1868. It was in that area and the year when Jemmie Kenney, an eight year old, was playing in the vicinity of school at the moment of insanity, an enormous eagle flew down, grabbed the boy with its powerful jaws, and then flew away together with Jemmie. According to the story that Jemmie's friends rushed in the building to inform the teacher about the attack however, when the teacher was outside, all he was able to be able to do was hear the devastated child's screaming as they flew away to the skies. The bird was apparently shocked by the sound and screaming of the children's classmates the huge bird landed on the child. The wounds caused by both talons and the fall were fatal to the victim.

In the 1940s, many reports of a massive raptor, which was as big as an aircraft, were reported within Alton, Illinois. A witness named EM Coleman who was one of the witnesses, described the raptor as "It was a massive extraordinary thing with a body, which resembled an underwater torpedo." Mr. Coleman would later add, "It was flying at approximately 500 feet, and cast shadow that was that was the same size as the shadow cast by a Piper Cub at that height."

Roc written by Edward Julius detmold

The two St. Louis policemen witnessed an identical-sized bird flying the same day. The officer Francis Hennelly stated, "It was as large as an aircraft of the size of a small one. The wings were flapping, and it was flying to the southwest, and was flying at an altitude of a few hundred feet. I was thinking it was an eagle of a huge size however, I've never seen one that large before."

On the 25th of July 1977, one of the most well-known modern-day encounters took place within Lawndale, Illinois. The incident has been featured on television shows, including Monster Quest.

It started innocently enough when ten-year-old Marlon Lowe was playing on the grass around his home. According to witnesses, two huge birds flew overhead. One of the huge raptors at the boy, and then grabbed his powerful talons, and then flew away with tiny Marlon in its midst. Astonished by what she just witnessed, Marlon's mom unleashed a blood-curdling scream when she pursued the massive bird and the child in distress. The massive bird let go of the 50-pound child, and then flew off to join its fellow. The terrifying attack in the morning was recorded by seven witnesses who provided the following summary description:

"It was white with a band around its half-foot long neck. The rest of its body was black. The bird's bill was 6 inches long and was hooked at the top. Its claws placed with three in front and one behind. Each wing, minus the body, measured four feet at minimum. The total distance of the bird's entire body from the beak to the tail feathers, was around four and a half feet."

Marlon as well as Ruth Lowe

The story was featured in national news. Afterward, the family faced constant teasing and ridicule. To prove the legitimacy incident, they solicited the assistance of two hunters from the area to try and take the birds down or kill them. The hunter's efforts failed.

To comprehend the Thunderbird To understand the Thunderbird, it is necessary to understand the perspectives of the individuals who are doing the reporting. They can mean something entirely different based on the lens through which they are viewed through. For certain people, Thunderbirds are spirit creatures who are devoted to everything that is pure. To others, they symbolize harbingers of changes, and there are people who believe that they are real creatures that swoop down on humans and take their carcasses to be eaten.

Perhaps no other cryptid in history has been so popularly embraced by numerous countries across North America. The name and the image of Thunderbirds are found on cars, hotels and sports teams, on TV shows and even on the U.S. Air Force's air demo team. The most intriguing question is what lies behind the mysterious trace of vapor left by Thunderbirds stories, legends and sightings.

Most reliable evidence: the large variety of sightings. Could they all be fakes or misidentified? The vast and extensive First Nation accounts of Thunderbirds all over North America certainly speaks to something amazing, either through oral tradition or myths and legends or perhaps something even more remarkable.

A reason to be skeptical To allow a bird to take a child in its arms it would have to be greater than those that are mentioned in the different incidents. An agitated raptor like the golden or bald Eagle is likely to hurt or even kill an individual in extraordinary circumstances, yet it is astonished by aerodynamics due to the size and dimensions given by the various witnesses to the numerous historical reports.

Jersey Devil

Locality: Pine Barrens of Southern New Jersey; Pennsylvania; Maryland and Delaware.

Description: A flying biped. The witnesses describe a creature that has the appearance of bats, leathery wings, cloven hooves, small arms sporting clawed hands, and a head that looks like an animal, with fiery-red eyes, horns and an elongated tail. The creature is described as making a roar and shrieking sounds.

The Jersey Devil is one of the most bizarre cryptids that can be imagined. It is said to have terrorized the Pine Barrens of Southern New Jersey since 1735.

Origin Story - Mother Leeds

Every great villain needs an engaging origin story for example, and Jersey Devil is no exception. What better place to begin with a dark and stormy night? This is precisely where we meet the poor mother of Leeds in 1735. To her utter dismay, Mother Leeds just discovered she was pregnant with the 13th of her children. After a moment filled with anger, Mother Leeds cries out at the sky, "If

I'm to have another child then let this one belong to Satan."

The majority of accounts show the baby born as a normal, beautiful boy, but soon upon birth, the infant magically transforms into a kangaroo like creature with clawed and small fingers, cloven hooves soft bat-like wings, an horned head of a goat and a sinister forked tail.

When it changed form into the creature the demon released an uncontrollable scream, which absolutely terrified all who heard it. Legend says that the beast killed the midwife , before climbing the chimney before disappearing in the darkness.

There is a claim that in 1740, clergymen fought this demon over 100 years. it was not seen again until 1890.

But, this doesn't help provide the explanation for the claim made by Joseph Bonaparte (Napoleon's older brother) who claimed to have seen the beast in 1820. Joseph claimed to have seen his first encounter with the Jersey Devil while hunting on his Borden town estate.

In the 1840s, the beast was reported to have killed animals in the region. The terrifying shrieks and groans were commonplace throughout the untamed Pine Barrens of Southern New Jersey.

The initial series of notable sightings during 1909, that publications and newspapers started referring to the animal as"the Jersey Devil. At this point, that the representation of the Jersey Devil develops.

The most famous encounters took place in the period between January 16 and 23rd, 1909. That was the week when The Jersey Devil attacked a trolley car that was crowded with passengers from Haddon Heights as well as members of a social group in Camden. Then, people on a trolley in Burlington claimed that the beast ran across the tracks just in front of the trolley. There was reports that police officers in Camden, New Jersey and Bristol, Pennsylvania shot at the beast, but had no impact on the beast.

The papers of the time were filled by stories of encounters reported with the demon monstrosity. The sightings were reported throughout the southern part of New Jersey down to Delaware and Western Maryland.

The fear spread so widely that certain Delaware Valley schools were closed and many people would not leave their homes due to the fear that they would be attacked, particularly those employed in the wood mills within and within in the Pine Barrens.

Strange tracks were discovered in the snow on fields, yards as well as on roofs of houses. Posses were created to guard an uneasy populace.

Firefighters in West Collingswood, New Jersey were summoned to the residence of one person who complained about that he had seen the Jersey Devil on his roof. As the firefighters switched their hoses towards the cryptid flying overhead the creature quickly attacked them before flying off.

In no way is it doubt that the reports of sightings and accounts about reports of Jersey Devil reached their peak during the January 1909 frenzies However, scores of sightings are still reported to this day.

In actual fact, in October of 2015, the famous flying cryptid became national and international headlines when Dave Black, a security guard, sent an image on his mobile phone to NJ.com which he had taken of the supposed Jersey Devil. He said the car he was driving to home came into view and the sighting was what he believed was an "llama" walking in the woodland.

In the words of Black, "I was just driving by Golf Course Galloway in Galloway on Route 9 and I was shaken several times when I was convinced that I had seen an animal called a llama. If it wasn't enough, it spread its wings in leather and flew away over the course. Perhaps my mind plays tricks with my mind, or I've just seen that the Jersey Devil. Thought I'd submit it to you for sharing. I'm not seeking any kind of reward, but wanted to see if someone else can clarify this with a rational fashion."

David Black's mobile phone photo from New Jersey Devil. New Jersey Devil

Though it's terrifying in terms of appearance and in its reputation, there is no other North American cryptid has been loved so much by those it terrorizes. It is featured on T-shirts, as a action figure, and perhaps as the name of NJ's NHL hockey squad.

Also known as Leeds Devil, Phantom of the Pines

Best evidence: The string of sightings which occurred during January 1909. The large amount of reported sightings occurred prior to any economic benefit due to the presence of a mysterious monster or cryptid.

The reason to be skeptical: The origin story is reminiscent of the many urban myths. But, it's also among the oldest recorded North American cryptids, so it's not difficult to imagine why it could be able to have so many different versions when it was passed down throughout the centuries.

Flatwoods Monster

Location: Flatwoods, West Virginia

Description The probe is described as extraterrestrial or alien. Around 12 feet tall with a dark-colored body and glowing eyes. The monster's head was described by witnesses as being elongated with huge eyes that sparkled and a unique head-shaped cowling that resembled an spade's ace. The arms were short and skinny with claws like hands, others claimed these features could be antennae. The creature or craft released the appearance of a mist, moved or floated above the ground , and was associated with a glowing red ball.

The whole thing began in the night on December 12, 1952. At around 7:15 p.m. Children witnessed the bright, pear-shaped object fly across the sky. It seemed to crash into an incline in the nearby farm. The thought was that it might be an aircraft that had crashed or possibly a UFO, the children called Kathleen May, mother of two of the boys who saw the trajectory of the object. Gene Lemon, an 18 year old West Virginia National Guardsmen, was in the company of his cousin Kathleen who was with the boys when they reported their incredible sighting. Along with the three kids who were watching the shining thing, Kathleen and Gene decided to take a look. The sighting was quickly was spread across the entire neighborhood. Then came another group of kids who ventured onto the land owned by local farm owner G. Bailey Fisher hoping to see what had fallen in the night sky.

They saw the 12 foot monster that was located about 100 meters away. As soon as the creature was conscious of the humans they were watching, it made an alarming sound, and then began floating towards the witnesses , covered in a peculiar fog. It released an unpleasant sulfur odor. The group was scared, and took off for the home of May She contacted her local Sheriff Department and the local newspaper to make a report about the incident.

Sheriff Robert Carr and Mr. A. Lee Stewert, co-owner of the Braxton Democrat conducted interviews with witnesses and visited the location with a teenager West Virginia National Guardsman, Gene Lemon, who was part of the group of witnesses who had seen the creature.

As they returned later in the evening they discovered that "there was a nauseating metallic, burnt, metallic smell persisting". Sheriff Carr along with the deputy Burnell Long went through the area in a separate search and found no evidence of the incident apart from the smell. The next day, at 6:45 a.m. The director for the regional Board of Education stated he saw an aircraft take off from the sky.

Further reports of encounters with this creature were reported. The mother of the young Guardsman claimed that at the moment of the collision, her home had been severely shaken and her radio was cut out for about 45 minutes.

The most alarming thing was the connection between those who viewed the creature, and then later became sick.

A number of members of the group who spotted the creature on the 12th of September were afflicted with symptoms such as irritation to the nose and inflammation of the throat. A lot of people attribute the health problems due to the strange mist that appeared to surround the creature. The symptoms seemed like those experienced by people exposed in the presence of mustard gas. The Guardsman was said to have problems following the incident with nausea and convulsions. Similar symptoms have been reported in those who suffer from hypersomnia.

The investigation revealed that one week before the incident on the 12th of September an adult mother and her daughter of adulthood claimed to have seen the same creature, and also reported the same strange smell. It affected her child enough that she was taken to the Clarksburg Hospital for three weeks.

Many speculate that the incident may have involved an extraterrestrial search and rescue operation. According to this hypothesis, we suggest they believe that Flatwoods Monster and its accompanying craft was stressed, and this triggered an UFO flap to rescue the both the vehicle and its owner.

Also called: Braxton County Monster, Phantom of Flatwoods, Lizard Monster, Green Monster

The best evidence: the number of witnesses, law enforcement mention of the peculiar metallic smell. Many UFO reports were reported around the date when the UFO sightings were reported. The sketches drawn by witnesses of the monster themselves are very consistent with the sightings of September 12th.

The reason to be skeptical: Similar to the reports of Mothman Some skeptics believe that it was a meteor paired with a misidentification of an owl. Both theories seem implausible because meteors rarely alter direction or slow to at speeds of less than 200 miles an hour. Also, those who live in the country do not tend to mistake smaller owls in 12 feet creatures. There are a few inconsistencies among the accounts of witnesses on whether the animal was armless or not, and whether the creature was real or a craft of some sort.

Chapter 10: Water

Cadborosaurus Willsi

Place: Cadboro Bay and Saanich Peninsula, British Columbia

Description: Sea Serpent. 20-40 feet long. The witnesses describe a head that resembles a horse big eyes, a long neck and small hind flippers. huge - possibly webbed - hind flippers and the tail is fan-shaped.

Over 300 hundred sightings over the past 200 years! The creature is described as traveling at speeds of up to 40 knots. The creature was reported to have been seen in the waters of the Pacific Northwest.

The name Caddy refers the town of Cadboro Bay in Greater Victoria, British Columbia. A description of the head-shaped horse of a serpent with big eyes and humps on its back, and a swathe of humps on its back, to Caddy and Nessie as well as Ogopogo (also mentioned by British Columbia).

A report from a couple of hunters for ducks, claimed that the creature had eaten their wounded ducks with its huge face and tooth-like saws.

Another fascinating report was reported in the month of October, 1937, when whalers from Naden Harbor Whaling Station in Vancouver were able to capture and kill the Sperm whale. After opening their stomachs, they were stunned to find what appeared to be the unidentified remains of a massive partly digested sea snake. There is no information on what was the fate of the creatures remains however, there is an interesting photo:

Mysterious remains have been discovered in the Sperm Whale believed to be the remains of an Cadborosaurus Willsi

Bob Iverson, Commercial Fisherman who lives on the shores of Cadboro Bay, spotted the animal from his backyard during the summer of 1997.

"It was extremely flat out there, the water was like mirrors. It was like a flash of light. on the opposite side of the bed of kelp there are four massive tires that seem like four large big truck tires. They come directly from the water. Then they fell after which they came up again, and they fell down once more."

Witnesses report the creature extending the head as well as body 12 feet from the water.

First Nation petroglyphs seem to depict similar creatures; One local island is referred to as"the Island of the Serpent.

Also known as Caddy

The best evidence: Kelly Nash video taken in 2009, depicts the large, multi-humped creature on the surface which appears to blow air out from its head. Photograph was taken by Naden Harbor Whaling Station.

Giant Oarfish

Be skeptical: Creatures frequently misidentified as Caddy including Sea lions and whales pipefish, basking sharks and giant Oarfish.

Ogopogo

The location: Lake Okanagan, British Columbia

Description: Lake Serpent. Around 40-50 feet long. A lot of lake monsters described as having green brown, black, or gray skin. The head of the beast is reported to differ greatly, with some comparing it to horses, camel, sheep, snake or seal. There are reports that say the snake's head has horns, that are external or physical ears. A few reports show the creature that resembles an Plesiosaurus.

Lake Okanagan is in British Columbia. The lake measures located in British Columbia. It is 84 miles (135 km) long and is between 2.5 to 3 miles (4 and 5 km) wide. It has the depth of an average 249 feet (76 m).

The rumors date back to around the turn of the century. There seems to be some connection with Ogopogo and the myths associated with First Nations reports of a water spirit known as N'ha-aitk or Naitaka who demanded an offering of a live animal to ensure the safety of the lake. State travelers were reported to sacrifice small animals, and then throw them in Lake Okanagan as an offering to the spirit in order to please the blood-sucking lake demon.

Monster Island

According to local legends according to local legend, the creature dwells in a cave beneath an island that is located in the lake. Since the beginning, people have believed the island "Monster Island" (also called Rattlesnake Island) contains the bones of the creatures' victims.

In 1926, at Okanagan Mission Beach, a sighting took place in which the passengers of around thirty vehicles were all able to see the creature.

A few cryptozoologists suggest that this creature found in Lake Okanagan is a form of a primitive serpentine whale, such as basilosaurus. This begs the question what if an air-breathing species which lived from 40 to 34 million years ago, in the latter part of the Eocene could be able to survive in a freshwater lake that has at times completely frozen?

Basilosaurus

It is possibly the most well-known of freshwater cryptids around the globe.

A woman from 1987, who wanted to go by the name Mrs. B. Clark, came forward to give an amazing story of their encounter with the beast thirteen years before. As an adolescent she was swimming towards an underwater platform roughly one-quarter of a mile away from shore when "something massive and heavy slammed into my legs." She was able to climb safely onto an oar while continuing to watch the creature. "I saw the hump, or coil, which was 8 feet long and four feet higher than the water surface, and was that was moving in a forward direction," said Clark. The creature was described by Clark as being between 25 and 30 feet long and dark gray in colour and sporting a whale-like tail that the long serpentine body acted as a huge inchworm.

Mrs. B. Clark's Sketch

One of the most well-known recent sightings took place in August 2008 along Highway 97 that runs between Peachland between Peachland and Summerland. Witness Sean Viloria in recounting his incident for an episode of Monster Quest, "I was stunned by the sighting, I was amazed...within minutes of seeing the creature, you can tell that it isn't supposed to exist."

Viloria was able to spot the creature along together with Jessica Weigers, who noticed an unusual disturbance on the surface of lake. Jessica remembers, "We were sitting in our favorite spot in the lake when I awoke and I noticed something moving through the trees. The thing I saw was two coils moving into and out of water, a snake-like body."

Sean adds "She was shouting and pointing at something she's spotted from the lake. I ran to her, and fell with my camera and I've got the creature completely in focus." That's the moment that Sean was able to take several photos of what people believe to be the mythical lake monster. The television series Monster Quest had the images independently evaluated and found no evidence of manipulation or hoaxing.

In the British Columbia newspaper article Viloria says, "Something is most definitely there, something completely unknown to science , that has found it's home Okanagan Lake. There are a myriad of possibilities for this to be true, and there is many evidences pointing to this. I believe it is definitely worthy of more attention by researchers."

Many people think that the photos that were taken by Sean Viloria on that August day were simply misinterpreted of a kite or possibly wind surfer. However, Sean would like to clarify that "I don't claim that I've taken a picture of an image of the Ogopogo in film. I'm merely saying I've snapped these photos of something tangible and moving, like a swimmer in the lake , and I'm not certain what they represent."

Also known as Naitaka (meaning "Lake Demon")

The most reliable evidence of 1926: At Okanagan Mission Beach a sighting was witnessed by approximately thirty vehicles were all able to see the creature.

Be skeptical: Many sightings could be explained by misrecognition of natural phenomena or animals. It's difficult to imagine an air-breathing plesiosaurus or basilosaurus living for long periods of time in a lake that is freshwater, particularly since it can be susceptible to freezing.

Champ

The location: Lake Champlain, Vermont, New York, US and Quebec, Canada.

Description: Lake Serpent. The lake monster is described by witnesses to be between 20 and eight feet in length. A serpentine, multi-humped body with an head that resembles the shape of a dog, snake or horse.

It is the 13th-largest lake of United States at roughly 490 square miles, Lake Champlain is 125 miles (201 km) in length, up to fourteen miles (23 km) across, and is the maximum in depth that is 400 feet (120 meters).

The myth of the large "horned serpent" lake monster dates back to the pre-European period of contact. The Iroquois as well as the Abenaki Native American tribes living close to Lake Champlain have legends regarding the creature. The Abenaki named the creature "Tatoskok" which means "great serpent" or "big serpent."

The waters around whether French explorationist Samuel De Champlain or a participant in his expedition saw the creature became very unclear. The story behind the legendary encounter with the explorer was revealed in an article in a 1970 issue of Vermont Life magazine by Marjorie Lansing

Porter. The article mentions that in 1609 when Champlain was exploring the lake, He observed "a serpent-like creature that was about twenty feet long, with a body as thick like a barrel, and having an head that resembled the head of a horse. But, there is no evidence that Champlain having ever written about an experience. It does seem to be an accurate description of Champlain explaining what sounds like an eel. In the course of this, Champlain stated that he saw the creature with "jaws of two foot and half long and a pair of sharp and deadly teeth. The body's shape likes the shape of a pike and it's armed by scales which a slash of the poniard dagger cannot penetrate the skin; and it is of silver grey color. The snout's point is similar to the snout of a hog. The fish is a threat to all the other fish in the rivers and lakes."

However, there are a multitude of photos of Champ to take into consideration. In 1870, people on steamboats located in Essex, New York watched in awe as they watched the neck and head rising from the water, leaving an unfathomably long wake of forty feet.

The following year, passengers on the steamship with a length of eighty feet Curlew saw the creature move in a "railroad speeds" and it was "strongly moved for 30 to forty feet away from the head of the beast while it was moving."

Another steamship named the W.B. Eddy was close to crashing after it was reported to have run into Champ.

The most famous sighting of Champ was in 1883, when the Sheriff Nathan H. Mooney proclaimed that he saw the sighting of a "gigantic water serpent that was about 50 yards" from the spot he was standing on the shoreline. Mooney added that he was close to the creature that he could see "round white spots in the mouth" and "the creature seemed to be approximately 25-30 feet long." As news of Mooney's sighting spread many eyewitnesses shared their stories of witnessing Champ, the Lake Monster.

The excitement over the creature may have reached its peak when none-other-than-famed self-promoter and showman P.T. Barnum entered the scene by offering an offer of $50,000 for the carcass of the beast!

In 1977, one of the most famous images of a cryptodism was captured by Sandra Mansi who was picnicking with her two children as well as her husband Tony on the shores of Lake Ontario.

Mansi Photo

Sandra recounts the incident to the series Unsolved Mysteries, "I'm looking out over the lake and the lake began to turn. The first thought I had was scuba divers, but it's too much, it'd be too large of a group of divers... Then I thought about fish, there's a very large sturgeon and massive walleyes in Champlain which is why I thought there's a large group of fish. The head and neck came out of the water to the rear and I watched it turn its neck, then take a look around. When it was first up its mouth was opened and I could see the water flowing from the mouth. I'm thinking that I shouldn't be there since I believe this creature should've been extinct for 30 million years ago. But still, I'm not afraid. I'm in complete awe, and extremely calm. And then Tony returned, and he noticed it, and then he went terrified and screaming and hollering. And he shouted at me to go back there and then he helped me get to the bank, and as he was done, I was handed the camera. I then returned and there. I grabbed the camera and took one photo."

The photograph became a news sensation. Both Life magazine and the New York Times and Life magazine report on the story. The subject in the photo appears to be plesiosaurus.

Ask Sandra Mansi whether she believes that Champ exists "You'll be unable to convince me otherwise. You can name it Champ and you can even refer to it as an monster...you could call it the plesiosaurus or you can name it whatever you like - I'm telling you, in the lake that there's something special."

The scientific backing of an unknown creature that lives in Lake Champlain, the echolocation recording from 2003 performed by the Fauna Communications Research Institute. Researchers recorded sounds with the characteristics to an orca or beluga whale but could not be identified with any known animal. Based on the findings of the scientists the unidentified creature's noise is likely to be mammalian since mammals are the only species that can echolocate.

Also known as Champy as well as the America's Loch Ness Monster, Tatoskok

Best Evidence: Echolocation recordings from the lake's interior at the Fauna Communications Research Institute in 2003.

Images of Echolocation of strange sounds recorded by Lake Champlain

The reason to be skeptical A reason to be skeptical: Large fish that are misidentified like the sturgeon, gar, or other species on the water, for example, swimming deer or Elk. Mansi negative photograph was destroyed and skeptical scientists say it may be just an image of floating log.

Altamaha-ha

Location: Altamaha River, Georgia

Description: River monster. About 15-30 feet long. It is described as with front seal-like flippers, with no back limbs, it propels itself into the ocean like a dolphin. It has a head that resembles snake, with a snout that resembles the crocodile.

Here's a New World cryptid with unique connections in The Old World's most well-known lake monster Loch Ness Monster. Loch Ness Monster.

On the shores of the 137-mile length Altamah River in Southern Georgia there is the old town located in Darien located in McIntosh County. Darien was initially created by Scot Highlanders who lived close to the famous Loch Ness. Actually, the town was initially named New Inverness.

It is believed that the Altamah River meanders through the center of one of the most affluent biological reserves within the Southern United States. The area is home to more than 100 endangered or rare species According to locals, it's the home to one huge swiftly moving river cryptid known as Altamaha-ha or Altie which is short for.

There are numerous accounts that suggest there was evidence that Tama Indians believed a giant serpent-like creature dwells in the Altamah River, but finding evidence of this claim was, again, as difficult as finding the creature itself.

One of the first reported reports of the creature became the subject of headlines in the April 22nd 1830 issue of the Savannah Georgian. In the story that follows, Captain Delano of the schooner, Eagle, claims that the monster was seen close to the mouth of the Altamaha River.

The article goes on to say, "He (Capt. Delano) repeatedly repeated the...particulars precisely in describing the animal that the man saw as approximately 70 feet long and the circumference of which was similar to the same size as the sugar hogshead (large barrel) that was being able to move with its head in the shape as an alligator's. It was about 8 feet from the waters."

Then Captain Delano made a statement against doubters that he may have had seen a whale, stating that "he has been exposed to every kind of whale and he has never seen more than once before...a creature similar as the whale (he) mentioned."

In 1981 , the creature became national headlines, after Larry Gwin, a former newspaper editor and his colleague, Steven Wilson, claimed that they had spotted a strange creature that had two large bumps that were about five feet apart. It produced a wake comparable to that of a speedboat.

The incident prompted other people to share their experiences with Altie. Like Harvey Blackman, who stated that he was able to see the creature during the 70s. The creature was about 15 feet in length and had a head that resembled a snake.

The sightings continue up to the present. There are several fascinating footage of an unidentified aquatic creature swimming, or scurrying through the channel of the river. There is a possibility that the Altamaha River remains one of the most magnificent, wilderness Rivers of the South, therefore it's possible that if there's a huge serpent river that is found located in North America, then the Altamaha River with its access to the Atlantic Ocean, might just be the ideal habitat.

Also known as Altie or the Monster of Darien

Best Evidence: Video captured close to Darien, at the Fort King George Historical site close to Darien. The tail that splashes towards the end of the video appears similar to that of the manatee.

There is reason to doubt is it because of immigrants Scot Highlanders creating the creature due to their cultural affinities with Nessie? The first modern sighting was recorded by a former newspaper editor that seems to be a fanciful coincidence. It is possible that manatees are misidentified as logs, dolphins, alligators and other natural objects and animals located in the region.

Loveland Frogman

The location: Loveland, Ohio

Description Humanoid Frog. Around three or 4 feet in height. The creature has been described by witnesses as bipedal and covered in the skin of a pale greenish-gray leather that has feet and hands that are webbed and a wide mouth , with sharp teeth.

Imagine driving along a rural road that is secluded in the dark of night. The road runs along the sloping contours of the Little Miami River near Loveland, Ohio. There aren't any other cars in the area at this time of night. When you come to a trough on the road, and suddenly you see three, almost amphibious humans, standing straight in a huddle by the edge on the roadway.

Based on the story of the Loveland Frogman this is precisely what transpired to an completely shocked and unidentified businessman in the month of May 1955. Evidently, he pulled up at near the edge of the roadway, and observed the creatures for about three minutes. The creature was described by the driver as being between three and 4 feet high, covered in light leather skin and webbed hands and feet, and was amazed by their distinctive "frog-like" head.

But, perhaps the most intriguing aspect of the incident happened at the exact moment the man was getting ready to leave He described how one of the creatures was holding an "wand" over its head. As it was doing so, sparks exploded from the device's bottom. That was enough of a reason for the businessman to smuggle it away.

The last confirmed sightings of the Loveland Frogman did not occur until almost 17 years later. At around at 1:00 a.m. on the 3rd of March 1972, a local police officer who was patrolling Riverside Road was heading toward the direction of Loveland when he came across what he initially believed to be a dog on the curb.

The animal jumped into the front of the patrol car, which forced the officer to apply the brakes on the frozen road. The "dog" started to rise on two feet and then turn in the direction of the police officer, focusing his attention. He later described how the upright frog like creature leapt over the guard rail and scurried down the embankment and going under the Little Miami River.

The officer estimated that the creature's weight to be between 50 and 75 pounds and was three to 4 feet high. The animal was described as having a skin that was leathery and said its appearance were similar to those of a frog. The next day, a second officer was dispatched to look into the incident and even though he didn't see any evidence that the animal was there, however, he did notice distinctive "scratch" scratches on the guardrail which the creature was said to have climbed up.

Two weeks later, Police officer Mark Mathews had an unusual incident that was very similar to the initial officer's encounter. Mathews, too, was driving his car in freezing conditions when he saw what he believed was an animal that was injured sitting on the pavement. Mathews left his car in order to take this animal off the road but when he walked up to the creature, it began to swell up and landed in an upright position. Matthews realized he wasn't dealing with an ordinary wounded animal. Incredulous at the bizarre lizard/frog-like posture, Mathews immediately took out his revolver, and fired shots towards the animal. The creature was able to climb the guardrail and was looking back at Mathews all the time.

Later, the officer Mathews was later to revise the more dramatic aspects of the encounter. In Mathews his revised account, he claims the animal is just a massive reptile, which probably ran away the owner. He stated that the reason to shoot at the creature was to show that the animal had a biological and very terrestrial ancestry. Only Mathews is able to determine the exact events that occurred during that cold, chilly day.

In 1972, another unknown farmer reported seeing four strange creatures roaming his fields, that were situated next to Little Miami River. The creature was described by the farmer as having pale greenish-gray skins and large, circular eyes as well as large mouths by sharp, pointed teeth. After the elusive Frogmen came aware of the presence of the farmer they quickly swam into the river , never to be observed for the rest of their lives.

Also known as Loveland Frog, Loveland Lizard

The Best Evidence What is the most convincing proof of the existence of this cryptid? Beats me. It's a difficult one to construct a compelling argument for, as our eyewitness evidence originates from an unnamed man in business as well as an unnamed farmer an unnamed police officer and finally an unnamed law enforcement officer who later changed his report. Although Carl Sagan acknowledged, "absence of evidence is not proof for absence" there does not appear to be enough evidence to prove the little guy's appearance as a frog.

When all is done and dusted it's difficult not to be a fan of the cryptid that has been the subject of a musical named after him , titled: Hot Damn! The Loveland Frog!

The reason to be skeptical: Eyewitness accounts with doubtful credibility as well as the insufficiency of reports of sightings.

Gold Country Bigfoot

My Bigfoot Encounter

Genetics, fate and a synchronicity of events caused me to experience an incredibly unexpected Bigfoot encounter. Because I am closely related to Daniel Boone (his mom was an Morgan) who was said to have recorded an Yahoo. My father was instrumental in arranging the way for Peter Byrne to have the benefit for the International Scouts which provided transportation for the Byrne's Bigfoot hunt team (see image below taken from the book by Bryne, The Search for Big Foot Monster, Myth or Man?)

International Scouts in front of The Bigfoot Information Center

As one of generation of baby boomers, I remember vividly the day Patterson-Gimlin Film became the subject of public notice. I can recall heated discussions with my friend who was trying convincing me that the actor could clearly see a zipper that proved it was a man dressed in a Bigfoot costume. It was a very heated debate. Legend of Boggy Creek and Chariots of the Gods were my top films growing up and I have never missed a single episode in In Search Of. It's difficult to understand the lack of documentaries available in the 1960s and in the early 1970s, besides National Geographic specials.

As Jane Goodall, I had always had a hankering that creatures such as Bigfoot existed, but I was able to moderate my romantic notions of the unknown with the sensible pragmatism of science that I found in books such as Carl Sagan's The Demon-Haunted World: Science as a Candle in the darkness.

In essence, until the day I first saw my first sighting I'd remained with an open mind in regards to possible Bigfoot's presence. In the event that I did have any hopes about the existence of Bigfoot then it was that if a convincing proof were discovered, it would be likely to establish that Bigfoot was a primate that had not been discovered or even a distant relative to man. However, that was going to be changed quickly (literally). When I encountered Bigfoot the way I conducted myself was totally out of character for me.

It was about the time of 4:30 p.m. on April 14, 2014. I was driving with my family as we went to visit my relatives within the Sierra Nevada Foothills. We were on a tiny rural road that I'd traveled numerous times over the course of my life since mid-1990s. situated in the middle of the state's Gold Country. Deer can be seen all the time present in the area. At the very least, a mountain lion regularly patrols the region, while occasionally, black bears have been seen from time to the.

We were laughing and smiling and just a little over a mile from where we were when we encountered the animal. When I made the corner, I saw an massive Sasquatch that was between eight and nine feet in height. It was just 50 feet away. This is where things go from bizarre to totally unfathomable. For the entire time it stared at me, I was unable to speak. as the speed of conversation slowed and my family continued to talk to each other, my wife sitting in the front seat, and my two children in my back.

Every person in the car must have witnessed the creature and was engaged in conversation. I ought to have stopped the car immediately because we had cameras on our phones however none of those thoughts were in my mind. What I did was continue watching the beast. The speed allowed is 20 miles per hour on this smoky single lane, once dirt road. I tried to slow the car but didn't stop. The creature took two massive strides to its right, towards the road. When there was a flash of yellowish-green light, and a puff , the creature vanished.

Slowly, the time began to get back to normal. I'm well-versed in this UFO phenomenon of missing screen memory and time and I immediately examined the clock in my car to ensure there was nothing missing. The time was 4:38 p.m. We were in the right place Thank God! My family was engaged in lively discussion and it was clear that none of them seen what I had just witnessed. In this moment, I was stunned in a state of confusion, unable to comprehend the incident that probably took just 10 minutes However, those 10 seconds changed my perception of the world.

Normally, I am friendly and sociable, however, following the incident I was surprisingly still. It took us only two minutes following my sightings to reach our destination. I quickly waved hellos to the family and then headed to the back of the house and gazed at the direction I was facing when I saw my sighting. Watching for any sounds and scouting the dark woods for strange movement, everything seemed to be normal. All was as normal at least except it was my sole passenger in the car who had just a few minutes earlier noticed to all intents and purposes, a massive large, hairy "Wookie" who gazed on me before disappearing in an instant of illumination.

I was sitting there reminiscing on what had happened I was in complete shock. The images repeated themselves in my mind. The colour of the creature was similar to greyish blue wet pine bark Massive lean muscle massive shoulders, a cone-shaped heads, and no head movement. My whole attention was centered on the dark eyes (the sun was still out and my car had its lighting for the day however there was no visible eye light) The creature was walking with a huge, relaxed stride. His lean and tall stature were staggering.

This is the first time I noticed the creature.

I didn't tell my family until a few months afterward. When I first reported my first sighting, California was experiencing one of its most severe droughts and the soil was extremely dry. In the case of the enormity of the creature, it'd be required to leave certain physical marks of its presence in the red and dry soil. I didn't search for tracks as I didn't want to explain my family members what I was doing, since I was unable to even imagine what I saw. For me I'm sure I saw something that was beyond the normal. The incident has caused me to have more questions than solutions.

Before sharing my story with my family, I shared my story to three of my closest acquaintances from the time I was a child. Although their advice was to simply leave it alone but it ignited my curiosity in the creature, and I began to research what other people were saying about. In my complete surprise, I soon learned of similar stories that described Bigfoot disappearing in the blink of a illumination! This was a feature of Bigfoot encounters that was completely undiscovered to me prior to my personal encounter.

The Bigfoot was right in front of the dark tree in the right image. He made a few steps, his height was approximately at the lower branch I am looking at , and then he disappeared from the point where I stand. To give the setting a measure, I'm 6 feet tall and have a weight of 220 pounds. The thing that is difficult to convey was the sheer weight of the beast. My estimation of my size in relation to Bigfoot I saw was the size of a five-year old, in relation to me in size.

When I was the subject of the incident, at the time of my sighting, I was aged 52, and in top health. I do not take any medication or consume any kind of recreational drugs, besides occasional booze (such like when I gather together with the same childhood buddies).

Applying Occam's razor analogy to show that the most simple answer is often the correct answer. My own ideas about Bigfoot after my personal bizarre encounter.

To comprehend the events that I observed they took me to ask myself, "What if they exist in a world that is different from ours?" Either as an interdimensional life form or an element of UFO mystery. The way Arthur C. Clarke stated, "Any sufficiently advanced technology can be distinguished from the magic of." The thing I witnessed on that day was nothing less than magical. It could also help clarify the greatest mystery surrounding the absence of an Bigfoot corpse ever getting discovered.

After my experience, have been absorbed in the of Bigfoot and know that every person has their own opinions on the nature of Bigfoot can or cannot be. I will not attempt to influence opinions in any way other that to clearly explain my experience in the best way of my memory.

My initial reaction when I saw the creature was thought it was shocked to see me. It appeared to be conscious and intelligent, since it immediately took action after spotting us coming. The most alarming and mysterious aspect of the encounter was the fact that my physiological and mental condition was actually affected directly by the presence of this creature.

As a passionate animal lover I've always an interest in the natural world for all of my life. My family and I visit the various zoos throughout California as well. I'm acquainted with the anatomy of primates as I have observed gorillas from the San Francisco Zoo and the Chimpanzees at the Oakland, Sacramento and Los Angeles Zoos. But, my observations and intuition kept saying, "This is not an unknown primate or human ancestor and is something that's completely different completely." There is absolutely no doubt that, if it wanted to hurt our species, it might probably done it, however, it chose to disappear.

To believe that it was a hallucination , would be just as amazing, considering it was the first within 52 trips around the sun. I've experienced no strange occurrences since the day I experienced it. While I enjoy exploring and learning about the unknown I do not want to go back to the same place only once in my life was enough.

There's never a moment which goes by without me thinking about this encounter. It remains for me an unanswerable mystery which has been a reminder of Shakespeare's famous quote in Hamlet, "There are more things in the earth and heaven, Horatio more than you can even dream of in your philosophical thought."

Chapter 11: Mysteries Of The Monkeys

The hat monsters live high up in the snowy peaks of the highest mountains on Earth? What weird and bizarre creatures are lurking in the dark corners of the world's jungles and forests? The 21st century isn't the only one, the planet is full of mysteries. The more we look into it the deeper we discover the little we know. The legends of legendary monsters are frequently exaggerated, however there are many who claim to have seen strange amazing creatures. These bizarre encounters have prompted many to look for evidence that the world's most mysterious creatures of mystery are real.

A performer portrays a Yeti.

Researchers who study cryptozoology are those who search for mysterious and undiscovered creatures. The name is derived to us from Greek word kryptos which translates to "hidden" also known as "secret," and "zoologist," which means "one who is a scientist who studies animals." They investigate the stories and myths of cryptids, animals who do not have enough evidence from science to show that they exist. The legendary man-beasts called Bigfoot as well as the Yeti are two examples of the creatures they are trying to locate.

Another kind of researcher is referred to as cryptobiologist. Cryptobiologists search for creatures that are not visible, looking for instances of species that were once thought to be extinct. Could Africa contain living dinosaurs in its forests? There is a theory that the Mokele-mbembe could be one of them.

It has been a few wins in the field of science that are looking for new as well as long gone species. Stories of the kraken, which is a huge squid has been shared by seafarers for centuries. In 1897 the body from one of the creatures was found in Anastasia Island off the coast of Florida. One hundred years later on the night of December 22nd the 22nd of December, 2006 an Japanese research team recorded the live squid. Scientists have now evidence that giant squids do exist and swim in the oceans of Earth.

Researchers from the field of cryptobiology were awestruck to find the coelacanth one of the fish that is believed to have died about 65 million years prior. It was discovered that the "extinct" species was alive and thriving through the water of Indian Ocean.

Coelacanth

It is hard to believe that in current times, there might be things that are not known to us. But, the universe is huge. There are parts of the jungle and mountains, forests and lakes that remain not explored. Are there any monsters in the area? Eyewitnesses say, "Yes!" Now the trick is to demonstrate that it is true.

2

THE YETI OR ABOMINABLE SNOWMAN

Y

Eti Abominable Snowman and Metoh-Kangmi, all are names that refer to a massive gorilla-like white creature believed to reside within the Himalayan Mountains. Yeti originates directly from Tibetan word yeh-the or "little human-like creature." The Sherpa language, the word "yeti," is understood to translate to "creature that lives in the glacier." From Western mountain climbers to the native Sherpas, Nepalese, and Tibetans, a lot of people believe that they have witnessed the creature or its footprints, which are found in snow.

Looking back at the earliest creatures that fit the description of the monster Cryptobiologists have pointed to the Gigantopithicus, which is a 10-foot (3-m) tall ape who was alive for millions of years before. The giant primate, thought to have died at the age of 100,000, is the ancestral ancestor of today's orangutans. Could a primate like this exist?

The idea of a huge Ape living in the top of a mountain is definitely fascinating. Many have sought out the mysterious yeti. It was 1953 when Edmund Hillary and his

Sherpa guide Tenzing Norgay were the first people to climb Mount Everest, the tallest ever climbed mountain on earth. While climbing Mount Everest they discovered remarkable footprints that were large within the snow. Hillary was perplexed. Which kind of animal would produce prints like this?

Seven years passed until the legend of mountain climbing returned to the region. He spent a decade searching for clues that could lead to the monster's existence. The year was 1960. Hillary tracked footprints heard stories from the locals and scoured the mountains hoping to locate a real live yeti.

Even though Hillary was unable to locate an actual specimen, he returned with possibly yeti fur as well as a scalp. Later tests confirmed that the fur was actually from an extremely very rare Tibetan blue bear. The hair that was kept in the Khumjung monastic site, turned out to be in fact the skin that was molded from serow, which is a kind of goat Himalayan antelope. The mountaineer was able to, however discover the reason behind the enormous tracks the climbers, as well as others were able to observe over the many years.

While on the mountain hunting, the team observed trails in the snow. In the event that the tracks were shaded they clearly resembled those of the fox. However, once the trail of a fox crossed into areas where sun shined down upon them the tracks were melted and transformed into long, human-like footprints. The repeated melting and refrefreezing of snow altered the tracks. If the footprints of a fox could stretch between 2 in (5 millimeters) to close to 1 foot (30.5 centimeters) It's not difficult to see how an even larger animal's prints could turn massive. Hillary was certain that the prints he'd seen in 1953 were probably created by a bear or perhaps a human climber.

Many have sought proof that the white gorilla-like beast called a yeti exists. The creature has not been discovered.

In spite of this that exists, many believe that some sort of creature lives in the Himalayas. Strange, high-pitched screams can be heard from the mountains, and locals speak of a formidable creature which could kill an ox in a single stroke of its muscled arm. Are the yetis really real? The existence of a massive creature found in the rugged glaciers of south Asia remains a mystery unsolved.

3

NORTH AMERICAN CRYPTIDS

T

They are referred to for their aliases such as Bigfoot, sasquatch, Fouke Monster, Momo, skunk Ape, and many other. All across all of the United States and Canada, there are tales of bizarre creatures described as a cross between human beings and giant Apes. They're almost always bipedal, walking on two legs , just like humans. Rarely seen, they believed to live in remote swamps and forests. They are generally described as being between 7 and 10-feet (2 to 3 meters) tall, and weigh up 500 to 500 pounds (227 kg). However, do they actually exist? Many witnesses have been reported, but scientists insist that they haven't found any human remains, or bones of the mysterious creatures.

Bigfoot/Sasquatch

Bigfoot/Sasquatch

Bigfoot refers to the name given to an animal that was spotted on the Pacific Northwest of North America. The name Bigfoot was coined by news reports about the creature's massive footprints. Another popular name of Bigfoot is sasquatch. It is an English variant of a term spoken by an Native American tribe called the Salish. According to the Salish language the word sesquac is a reference to "wild human."

In 1995 in 1995, The Bigfoot Field Researchers Organization (BFRO) was formed to research the mystery creature. BFRO has recorded numerous sightings. From hikers and campers to park rangers, scientists and rangers, many individuals claim to have encountered an enormous animal that is hairy. For proof of this, there are plaster castings of footprints, recordings the sound of screeching or howling as well as blurred photos and movies. However, actual encounters are often masked by fakes.

Dale Lee Wallace holds a tomper the uncle of his, Ray Wallace, used to make the huge footprints that were discovered in the northern California log camp in the year 1958.

The year was 1958. Ray Wallace created a Bigfoot sensation after he claimed to have discovered footprints that were large in the northern California log camp. Through the decades, Wallace became known as the "Father of Bigfoot." It was not until Wallace's passing on November 2, 2002, that the family uncovered an unfinished pair of wooden feet Wallace was able to use to create the large footprints. The joke was a viral sensation that the joker didn't anticipate. He kept it a secret until his death when his family discovered the wooden stompers in Wallace's possessions. The truth is, BFRO researchers have examined castings of plaster that were made of those feet, and also castings of the original footprints in 1958. They believe that both prints do not coincide. Only Wallace could be the only one to know for certain but he is unable to anymore.

The film from 1967 by Patterson and Gimlin seemed to confirm the existence of Bigfoot was real until the person in the costume admitted to having been tricked.

The most well-known source of evidence is a film in the year 1967 made by Bigfoot seeker Roger Patterson and Bob Gimlin. They had traveled to Bluff Creek, California, an area known for its footprints and sightings. They were determined to capture an image of a Bigfoot onto film. They achieved this by bringing back footage of a beast walking, looking at the camera, turning before walking away. For more than 35 years, the footage appeared to be an actual proof till Bob Heironimus came forward. Bob claimed at the time he was just 26 at the time and was commissioned from Patterson along with Gimlin to dress in an altered great-ape costume. The footage appeared to indicate that it was not real. But, BFRO questioned Bob's confession. BFRO stated that the initial Bigfoot costume has not been discovered and no one has been successful in replicating the costume with accuracy, though numerous sources have attempted.

Is the mysterious Bigfoot exists? If there is any evidence or not, there are plenty of eyewitnesses that claim something of a creature is out there.

Fouke Monster

The tiny community located in Fouke, Arkansas, is reported to be home to a legend 7-foot (6-m) tall hairy monster with a penchant for sheep, cows, and chickens. It was in the late 1970s that the city gained national attention when a newspaper journalist Jim Powell wrote about members of a family in the town who were scared by"the "Fouke The Monster."

The story goes that the resident Bobby Ford had just returned to his home after a hunting trip in the month of May. The two of them believed they had seen something in the rear of his home. Utilizing a flashlight, men were able to spot a creature. The shots were fired. The men believed that the animal was falling but when they began to walk toward it when a female's shouts cut them.

Hearing the screams of the wife Ford was racing to get to her front lawn. He was not expecting to encounter an enormous creature with eyes that were red. The beast attacked, wrapping its savage arm around Ford's shoulders and neck. Furious, Ford was able to break free and ran at in full speed through the front door. There was his wife, Elizabeth who was terrified after seeing the beast's clawed hand reach for an unlocked window. The Fords immediately contacted the sheriff's department in the town.

A thorough investigation was conducted, especially in the vicinity where men believed they had killed the animal. The body was not found, nor any blood, was discovered. However, they did notice some strange tracks on the ground and a few damaged branches of trees and claw marks on the front porch. The Fords were scared to remain in their house. Within a couple of days they left.

The story was picked up by national media. Monster hunters, researchers and journalists all travelled to Fouke to interview local residents as well as exploring the region. The rewards were given to those who could locate the creature. The rewards never came in However, a film was made. The Legend of Boggy Creek Part documentary and part fiction, was released in theaters in 1973.

There are some who wonder whether the man who attacked Bobby Ford was a bear or maybe the mountain or a lion. Some believe it was an elaborate prank. Some believe that the Bigfoot-like creature actually observed. Leslie Greer, who was the county sheriff from 1967 until 1974, reported a number of reports of sightings of creatures. In an interview with him, he stated, "I don't know what they were seeing, but I believe that they witnessed something."

Momo

The Missouri Monster or Momo appears to be a bigfoot like creature, reportedly living on the Mississippi River in Missouri. The smelly, hairy cryptid was first seen in the 1970s early. On the 11th of July in 1972, it came to the attention of the world after it came close to the Harrison family's residence outside of the city in Louisiana, Missouri.

The day was a hazy one. Terry as well as Wally Harrison, ages 8 and five, were playing in their backyard. The two boys heard a rumbling then looked to find an enormous creature that was covered in blood, and carrying dead dogs. Their screams could be heard by their elder sibling, Doris, who was in the house.

Through a window, she saw Momo standing in front of an oak tree. Doris spoke of the creature as: "Six or seven feet tall, hairy and black. It resembled an adult, but it didn't appear as if it was." The children were able to escape while the cops were summoned.

In the following days, people also were able to hear loud growling noises. They also noticed an odd, unpleasant smell which Edgar Harrison, the children's father, described as "a stinky horse scent or a strong smell of garbage."

On the 19th of July, Police Chief Shelby Ward and 18 others searched thoroughly the area. The area was not searched for. The next day, the reporter was escorted by Edgar further up the hill. There , they found 10 inches (25-cm) footprint, as well as what was believed to be a five-inch (13-cm) footprint. They decided to look for an abandoned, rundown shack which Harrison believed could be a suitable place to rest in the case of the Momo. In the shack, they were awed by the stench of a terrible odor. Harrison was certain that the creature was in the vicinity. However, even after they immediately went to the area and searched however, they could not find anything.

As time passed, many other witnesses have reported seeing the creature. Cryptozoologists were everywhere as did TV and journalists from newspapers. Eyewitnesses were interviewed repeatedly. They told of a 6' (2-m) tall creature with long black hair. The head appeared to rest straight on its shoulders like it didn't have a neck.

Unfortunately, there was never discovered to prove its existence. Further sightings were reported over the time. Many agree that the number of eyewitness accounts are not to be discounted However, what exactly they witnessed remains an unanswered question.

Skunk Ape

The Florida Everglades are home to a species which has been dubbed the Skunk ape. The Bigfoot-like creature has been described as a huge gorilla- or orangutan-like creature with a foul skunky smell.

A picture of the "skunk Ape" handed by the Sarasota County Sheriff's Department.

While the animal had been observed since the 1940s the skunk was the subject of much attention on the 22nd of December 2000. On the 22nd of December it was reported that it was reported that the Sarasota County Sheriff's Department received an email and photos from an old woman who had captured photos of the skunk ape in her backyard a few weeks prior. Her husband was of the opinion that the creature could be an orangutan. She was worried that it was the pet of a family member that got loose.

The animal smelled disgusting and appeared to be hungry since it snatched apples from the basket that the woman kept in her backyard. Since it was this big the woman was worried that it could attack anyone. She said, "...I judge it to be about six and a quarter to seven feet tall. ...." The lady continued to talk about the general area she was and requested for the police to begin looking to find the creature.

The police started looking for. They issued a caution to the residents to be cautious around the animal. They believed that they were searching for an orangutan of a huge size. But the moment the local Cryptozoologist Chris Dotson saw the pictures and realized that they were searching for something twice the size of an orangutan. He believed it was a skunk. Dotson said, "People need to stay clear of it and let experts to enter the scene with some understanding of big primates such as this and then trap the animal."

Unfortunately, whether it was an orangutan, skunk, or an ape, the animal was not found. Other reports of a large creature found in Florida continued. What did it look like? It's an unanswered question.

Conclusion

The majority of species studied by scientists are described as cryptids in some time in the past. Giant squids are an excellent illustration, as is the vampire bat. Both were extensively discussed however zoologists dismissed them as myths. In the end, however the evidence was substantiated and scientists accepted them as true. It is what will be the case for some cryptozoa in this book. In the case of others, an alternative explanation could be provided. It could be a mix-up of two distinct creatures, such as the Chupacabra. It could be a biological process that causes bizarre and terrifying hallucinations similar to the hag or the incubus. There could be a myriad of explanations to explain the myth of the cryptid. However, most of the time, that explanation is actually a real animal that is or a variation of an animal that is well-known or, if it's rare, excitingly an entirely new animal to scientists.

It's this possibility that keeps drawing people into the cryptozoology field - the thought that you might be the person to prove the existence of an undiscovered creature. It's a field full of hoaxers and cranks however there are many genuine committed and competent people as well. The positive side lies in the fact that technology has made it simpler to participate and aid in making real discoveries. You don't have to spend the cash to make an excursion to a remote or even dangerous location and by looking through stories from folklore, field reports, and scientific journals, you can to find patterns, establish connections and play a crucial role in solving a mystery. It's also simple for cryptozoologists to publish information that would not be considered appropriate for a conventional journal, which means there's more data to analyze than previously.

If you're interested by any of the cryptids discussed in this book, you'll be able to quickly begin to investigate them yourself. The reference list is a good starting point , but there's plenty more online, which ranges from the most outrageous conspiratorial theories, to research research papers and diaries from famous scientists. Nothing is new; many people have read it and thought about it before . However, it might be that a key connection is there, and no one has noticed it until now. The answer to every scientific puzzle was all around until someone came across it to it, and cryptozoology isn't any different. If you can debunk an untruth or draw connections between the research report and an local myth, it's a significant contribution. It's possible that you'll find solid evidence that a cryptid is real.

Since some have. There have been numerous instances of legendary animals that turn into real and real for one to rule out it without a second thought. Humans have spread across the globe, however there are vast areas particularly in the rain forests and in the deeps in the oceans, where humans is not so much. The enormous squid and the goblin shark show that massive animals are able to exist without any discovery for a long period of time. It's impossible to believe that we've found all the things we can find.

This book has intentionally steered away from anything that could be believed to be hoax (with only Elwetritsch) and has focused on cryptids that have long and storied history, backed by numerous independent sources. They're those that are most likely to have a foundation in fact. From Percy Fawcett's gigantic anaconda to the massive sharks seen off Australia by many sailors, those are all animals that are probably present in the form of. They may not be as large as people claim. They might be a species that's grown to a size that's unusually large or simply viewed in poor light or at an angle that is unusual. It's possible that they may be the only thing that's been reported.